BRAVELY

> "The best protector any woman can have,
> one that will serve her at all times and
> in all places, is courage."

ELIZABETH CADY STANTON
SUFFRAGIST

We began researching and writing *Bravely* to herald a major
milestone in the ongoing push for equal rights: the centennial of
the Nineteenth Amendment's addition to the US Constitution.
We completed it in the midst of another historic call to courage:
the global coronavirus pandemic.

We dedicate this book to the dreamers, doers & defenders
whose personal bravery and collective endeavors have
valiantly moved the world forward.

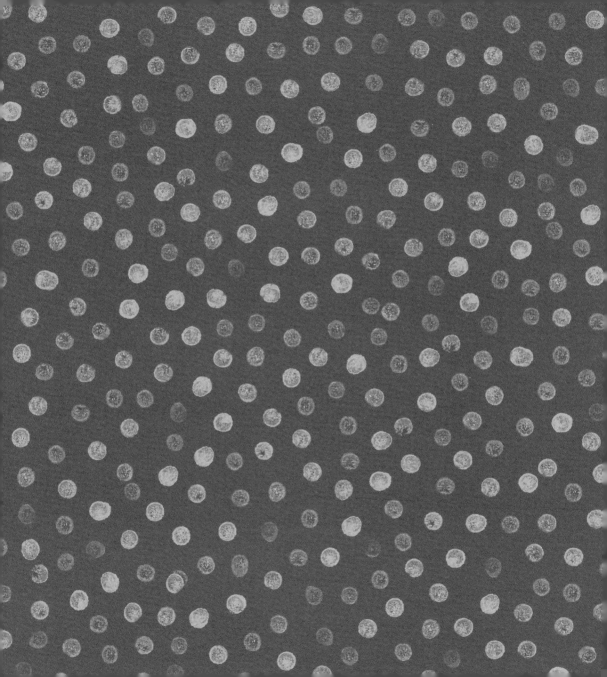

BRAVELY

INSPIRING QUOTES & STORIES FROM
TRAILBLAZING AMERICAN WOMEN

RUNNING PRESS

PHILADELPHIA

Running Press
Hachette Book Group
1290 Avenue of the Americas, New York, NY 10104
www.runningpress.com
@Running_Press

Printed in Singapore

First Edition: March 2021

Published by Running Press, an imprint of Perseus Books, LLC, a subsidiary of Hachette Book Group, Inc. The Running Press name and logo is a trademark of the Hachette Book Group.

The Hachette Speakers Bureau provides a wide range of authors for speaking events.
To find out more, go to www.hachettespeakersbureau.com or call (866) 376-6591.

The publisher is not responsible for websites (or their content) that are not owned by the publisher.

Print book cover and interior design by Frances J. Soo Ping Chow.
Patterns copyright © Getty Photos

Library of Congress Control Number: 2020935033

ISBNs: 978-0-7624-7151-5 (hardcover), 978-0-7624-7150-8 (ebook)

COS

10 9 8 7 6 5 4 3 2 1

CONTENTS

THE QUOTEUR LIST

quoteur / KWÖ TƏR
A person who originates a collection of words worth sharing

IDEAS & STORIES TO INSPIRE
A FUTURE BEYOND

This book is brimming with ideas and stories of women—pioneers of possibility—who, in ways simple and profound, have left their mark across all fifty US states. Builders, dreamers, and intrepid leaders, they represent the best of a nation shaped by a promise and filled with hope. In finding their place—and helping others find theirs—they allow us to see many paths forward.

Throughout these pages you'll discover quoteurs past and present, some well-known and some not yet discovered but worthy for sure. In their words are uncommon insights, plainspoken thinking, and wisdom packed with layers of meaning. Some quotes speak to moments of reckoning for those who persevered through unthinkable circumstances or who let serendipitous happenings re-steer their course. Other ideas emerged as people set out to pursue a grand vision or defend an ideal.

All of these stories remind us that destiny is not preordained.

Alongside pioneering artists, scientists, politicians, farmers, movement-sparkers, and self-made billionaires, you'll find the world's most widely syndicated columnist, the original software engineer, classical music's debut maestra, and even the National Park Service's earliest "lady lookout." Besides scouting fascinating female firsts, we've handpicked stories that connect to beloved American institutions, from the Statue of Liberty to the Hollywood Walk of Fame, the Kentucky Derby to the Wild West, Thanksgiving feasts to Southern soul food.

So drift through the pages. Linger on words. Delve into stories. Get riled up. Cherish what's nostalgic. You might uncover a catalyst to reinvigorate your thinking or a dose of timely inspiration that will lift someone you know.

Fixing the Quote Supply Problem

Since stumbling upon the world of quotations, we've developed a fascination bordering on obsession with the power that's packed in just a few short words. Yet the words of women often remain undiscovered, misattributed, unsourced, and simply absent. For every amazing historymaker whose ideas we've been able to recover, there are so many more whose voices are sadly lost forever.

We're steadfast in our mission: to fix the quote supply problem so an abundance of ideas, which are a gateway to rich stories, become visible. Beyond our books and products-for-good, we continue to gather and share thousands of sourced quotations through our digital destination Quotabelle.com.

As research aficionados and dedicated "cite-seers," we've had ahas! along the way. This book, *Bravely,* came from one of those moments.

The United States, in so many ways, has been built upon the efforts of strong women. But scour the many history books, rousing presentations, thought-provoking articles, leadership publications, social media posts, and inspirational goods out there and you'll discover that the core principles we hold in high esteem (like honor, valor, innovation, and freedom) are missing meaningful—or even passing—references to women. We're setting out to change that by adding missing voices back into history and ensuring today's leading lights don't go overlooked.

On This Journey Together

Our hope is that teachers, leaders, and students—frankly, all of us—are inspired to share the thinking of remarkable women & girls so more role models emerge.

And, we hope this book will help you find muses on whose shoulders you can stand and lean as you bravely chase the future with courage and grit and kindness and honor and humanity.

CHEERS!
PAULINE & ALICIA

AUTHENTICALLY

"True belonging doesn't require you to change
who you are. It requires you to be who you are."

BRENÉ BROWN
SOCIAL WORKER

Sarah Josepha Hale

1788–1879

EMINENT WRITER • US'S 1ST FEMALE MAGAZINE EDITOR •
"MOTHER OF THANKSGIVING"

When Sarah Josepha Hale was widowed at 44, she suddenly had to find a way to support her five children. The self-taught Sarah opted to write, eventually becoming a leading author who used her pen for far more than simply making a living. Starting off with children's poetry, Sarah had an instant hit with the now classic nursery rhyme "Mary Had a Little Lamb" (which became the first speech recorded on Thomas Edison's newly invented phonograph). The success of her debut novel *Northwood* grabbed the attention of a women's magazine owner, launching Sarah's career as an "editress." During her 40 years at the helm of *Godey's Lady Book*, Sarah used the wildly popular periodical as a platform for an agenda that mixed staunchly traditional and surprisingly modern values, always with a healthy dose of religion. While unflaggingly promoting women's domestic duties, the tried-and-true campaigner backed abolition, pay equity, and women's education. She also pushed for the preservation of George Washington's historic home of Mount Vernon and even got the word "Female" removed from the name for Vassar College in 1867.

Today, Sarah is best remembered for her 36-year personal crusade to establish Thanksgiving as a national holiday. The New England folk tradition was dear to her heart. Besides expressing gratitude for the bounty of the land, it paid tribute to community and "the wealth of home." Her writings publicized the event with quaint accounts of the festivities and mouthwatering recipes for what would become beloved standards, including the "lordly" roasted turkey and custardy pumpkin pie. After decades of her penning thousands of letters to leaders and lobbying five presidents, it was Abraham Lincoln who finally made Thanksgiving official in 1863. His proclamation, influenced by the desire to reunite a country torn apart by the Civil War, made it one of the four original federal holidays, including Christmas, New Year's, and the Fourth of July. The beloved annual festivity has been on the books ever since . . . and we have Sarah to thank for it.

The good, the true,
the tender, these form
the wealth of home.

SARAH JOSEPHA HALE
EDITOR

Annie Oakley

1860–1926

CHAMPION SHARPSHOOTER • BUFFALO BILL HEADLINER • AMERICA'S 1ST FEMALE SUPERSTAR

Phoebe Ann Mosey took her first shot with her father's old rifle at age eight, landing a squirrel. Her dad had died two years earlier, leaving Annie, her mother, and six siblings to fend for themselves in an Ohio cabin. Annie's talent soon became the ticket to the family's survival. The little sure-shot supported them with hunting and trapping. By age 15, she had paid off her mom's mortgage by selling small game to a local grocery store. The same year, Annie famously bested a seasoned pro, Frank Butler, in a Cincinnati shooting competition. Frank wasn't a sore loser. He would become her husband, performing partner, and manager on the show circuit. Though entranced by her unrivaled skills and charm, Frank hadn't intended to help showcase them. When his longtime performing partner fell ill, Annie filled in, instantly winning over the crowd. Annie Oakley was born.

Recruited by Buffalo Bill Cody, she became a feature act of his namesake show *Buffalo Bill's Wild West and Congress of Rough Riders of the World*. Under the billing of "Peerless Lady Wing Shot," she toured the US and Europe for 17 years, wowing crowds, royalty, and heads of state while becoming fast-and-thick friends with the celebrated Lakota Sioux chief Sitting Bull. Annie would split the thin side of a playing card, hit targets behind her using only a mirror, and knock ashes off a lit cigarette hanging from her husband's mouth. Then, the 5-foot-tall wonder in skirts and a Stetson hat would winningly skip offstage. Shooting only for survival and show, she never took aim at a human and, contrary to many other Wild West women, lived like a proper Victorian lady outside her public persona. Annie carried on training up future markswomen and doing charity exhibitions well into retirement, notching her last record just two years before her death. Her legend continues to hit the high mark in pop culture, with biographical films, TV shows, and even a Broadway musical.

"

Aim for the high mark, and you will hit it.

"

ANNIE OAKLEY
WILD WEST PERFORMER

Edna Lewis

1916–2006

For young Edna Lewis, farm-to-table eating wasn't a culinary or lifestyle choice, it was her entire way of life—necessary and demanding but also inspiring and creative. She grew up in Freetown, Virginia, an agricultural community of freed slaves and their families cofounded by her grandfather. The entire town worked together to achieve self-sufficiency while celebrating their land and heritage. They planted, harvested, hunted, and foraged every ingredient that went into what they ate—not only biscuits, fried chicken, and greens, but herring roe and deviled crabs, potted guinea hen and turtle stew, watercress and wild asparagus, brandied peaches and blackberry wine. Edna was the first to bring an intimate portrait of this authentic Southern food culture to a nationwide audience. Today, her artful preservation of traditional folkways has become the foundation of one of the US's most distinctive cuisines.

Edna left Freetown for the urban North after her father died during the Great Depression. The teen found work as an expert seamstress in New York City, eventually attracting an elite clientele for her replica designer dresses and Africa-inspired fashion. As her food became the stuff of local legend, she returned to her culinary roots. In 1948, she partnered with a friend to open a bistro on Manhattan's East Side. Her menus made Café Nicholson a celebrity favorite, drawing in diners from Eleanor Roosevelt to Marlene Dietrich and counting Truman Capote and Tennessee Williams as regulars. As one of the first renowned female chefs, Edna would go on to head fine-dining kitchens up and down the Eastern Seaboard and pen influential cookbooks. Her 1976 classic, *The Taste of Country Cooking*, combined recipes with memoir to faithfully capture the flavors and philosophies of the dishes she learned cooking with her Aunt Jenny over a wood-fired stove. The first recipient of the James Beard Living Legend Award, Edna's still considered a giant of American cookery. Her story has inspired a novel, one-woman show, and nonprofit dedicated to reviving African American food history.

The secret is in the ingredients.

,,

EDNA LEWIS
CHEF

Amy Gulick

born 1965

AUTHOR • VISUAL STORYTELLER • MIDWESTERNER
INSPIRED BY ALASKA'S RAREST ECOSYSTEMS

Amy Gulick undertook her first major nature photography project in 2001—a monthlong sojourn to the Arctic National Wildlife Refuge, when it was under threat of oil drilling. She had to use a clunky satellite phone to upload tiny, grainy images for each of her daily web posts. A writer-photographer who had been honing her craft since high school, Amy long recognized the power of combining words and images to tell impactful stories. A born nature lover, she spent much of her childhood tailing frogs and fireflies and knew she wanted to use her gift for visual storytelling in the service of the environment. Despite technical constraints, Amy found that sharing the rugged beauty of the remote Alaskan refuge made a difference. Her stories stuck with people in a way that facts alone did not and helped turn the tide of public opinion, putting a halt to a government policy that would open protected lands to development. Since then, the award-winning photographer has kept her eye on the "big picture" by focusing on endangered species, old-growth forests, the illegal wildlife trade, and plastics in the oceans.

Today, Amy's beloved Arctic Refuge is once again in imminent danger. She is facing new challenges, too: with a never-ending stream of content, how do you capture people's attention long enough to win their hearts? Picking wonder-sparking subjects has helped—like her multimedia exploration of the unexpected eco-interdependencies between seagoing salmon and the inland trees of Alaska's Tongass Rain Forest. Not only do the intrepid fish rely on trees to protect their spawning zones, the remains of millions of salmon caught by bears end up fertilizing the forest floor. While she's partnered with multiple nonprofits and NGOs, from The Nature Conservancy to the Sierra Club, to amplify her messages, she's also remained strategically independent. Committed to "honest documentary," Amy reaches a wider audience by offering people a new perspective without telling them what to see.

> **Capture the heart, and the mind will follow. Change the mind, and change the conversation.**

AMY GULICK
CONSERVATION PHOTOGRAPHER

America Ferrera

born 1984

AMBITIOUS KID ACTOR • 1ST LATINA TO WIN A LEAD ACTRESS EMMY • INVENTIVE CONVERSATION-CHANGER

America Ferrera always knew she wanted to act. She auditioned for a junior high production of *Romeo & Juliet* as a third-grader, saved up her babysitting money to take acting lessons, and signed with an agent as a teen. It was an aspiration discouraged by her friends, family, and teachers, who knew that girls with her background—the daughter of Honduran immigrants—were often consigned to cookie-cutter stereotypes and background scenery. As she kept getting calls to play parts like "sassy shoplifter" or "pregnant chola #2" and hearing from casting directors that she was "too specifically ethnic" for meatier roles, America tried to conform to Hollywood expectations. But her first title role in the 2002 film *Real Women Have Curves* required her to be herself—her authentic, poor, curvy, Latina self. The movie was a hit and her subsequent primetime series *Ugly Betty* got 11 Emmy noms in its first season and nabbed America a Golden Globe. Girls were inspired after finally seeing themselves represented on the big and little screens. A young Malala Yousafsai even revealed that a stack of *Ugly Betty* DVDs lit her dream of becoming a journalist. Yet, America didn't see the cultural sea change she expected—an opening up to diverse experiences reflecting how the world really looks.

America decided to take the narrative into her own hands. Besides establishing her own production company, she cofounded the nonprofit Harness as a forum where grassroots leaders collaborate with pop culture influencers to shift the public conversation around hot-button issues. The group has livestreamed a dinner party of activists hosted by Katy Perry, gotten a network's worth of showrunners to sit down with community-based advocates, and partnered with digital media outlets to spotlight contemporary changemakers. Recently, the coincidentally named America curated *American Like Me*. The best-selling collection of personal essays shares the stories of people like her, who embody the US's multicultural identity.

The truth is,
I am what the world
looks like.

"

AMERICA FERRERA
ACTOR

BOLDLY

"It's easier to beg forgiveness
than it is to ask permission."

GRACE HOPPER
COMPUTER SCIENTIST

Bessie Smith

1894–1937

VAUDEVILLE PERFORMER • HIGHEST-PAID
BLACK ENTERTAINER • "EMPRESS OF THE BLUES"

A pioneer and popularizer of the blues, Bessie Smith was an icon in her day. At the height of her popularity in the 1920s, she sold millions of records, sang to standing-room-only houses wherever she went, and was an in-demand collaborator with jazz greats like Benny Goodman and Louis Armstrong. Her singularly bold style set the stage for divas like Billie Holiday, Aretha Franklin, and Janis Joplin (who would one day help pay for her headstone). Bessie's hypnotizing performances were famous for making people laugh and cry over the course of the same song as she retooled melodies to tell each story her own way. Those stories were not just about grief and loss, but also independence and empowerment.

The deep feeling and fight in her persona came from someplace real. Bessie was born into poverty, but things got worse when both of her parents died by the time she was 10. Her older sister took in laundry to keep the family from starvation. Bessie knew her voice was the only way out. She had already worked up a local following around Chattanooga churches when, at 16, she was taken under the wing of blues singer Ma Rainey and joined a touring minstrel show. Ten years later, in 1923, she was signed by Columbia Records. Her first release—her take on "Downhearted Blues"—was an instant hit, selling 780,000 copies in six months. Even in her heyday, life was no cakewalk for the Empress of the Blues. She confronted discrimination, was cheated out of royalties, and was rocked by stormy love affairs. When she died in a car crash, 5,000 people attended her Philly funeral, yet her grave remained unmarked for more than 30 years. Today, Bessie is heralded for her role in shaping the country's sound heritage. A Grammy Hall-of-Famer, her music has been singled out for preservation by the Library of Congress's National Recording Registry.

" I don't want no drummer. I set the tempo. "

BESSIE SMITH
SINGER

Patsy Takemoto Mink

1927–2002

LAWYER • 1ST WOMAN OF COLOR ELECTED TO US CONGRESS • EQUAL-OPPORTUNITY POWERHOUSE

Patsy Mink consistently and unflinchingly lived her life ahead of the majority, pushing for the more equitable world she wanted to see. When she arrived at college in Nebraska to find that all minority and international students were assigned to a single dorm and barred from the Greek system, she led a successful fight to end the segregation of campus housing. When no medical school would accept her, she found her place at the University of Chicago's Law School. When no law firm would hire her after she became the first Japanese American woman to pass the bar in Hawaii, she started her own private practice, catering to clients denied service by established outfits. When her state party deemed her "unelectable" and regularly refused to back her candidacy for local and federal offices, she ran her own grassroots election campaigns.

Being ahead of the majority means you can't always win. In addition to disheartening defeats in mayoral, gubernatorial, senate, and even presidential races over the course of her career, Patsy lost her first bid for the US House of Representatives after Hawaii became a state in 1959. When she finally won her seat in 1964, she served six consecutive terms and returned for six more in the 1990s. She was still on the ballot following her sudden death in 2002 and was posthumously reelected by a landslide. Being a visionary in Congress meant that much of the legislation she sponsored never made it on the books. Bills to establish a comprehensive early childhood education system, create affordable childcare, and withdraw troops from Vietnam were voted down or vetoed. Yet, she pulled off epic victories we're still benefiting from today, including as a principal author of Title IX. Passed in 1972, the revolutionary law banned sex discrimination in any educational program receiving federal funding. Officially renamed the Patsy T. Mink Equal Opportunity in Education Act, it created parity in admissions, scholarships, curricula, faculty hires, and athletics—girls' participation in sports alone has soared from 300 thousand to 3 million since.

"It is easy enough to consistently be with the majority. But it is more often more important to be ahead of the majority."

PATSY MINK
CONGRESSPERSON

Joan Ganz Cooney

born 1929

PUBLICIST & PRODUCER • EDUCATIONAL TV TRAILBLAZER •
"CRUSADER AT HEART" BUSINESSWOMAN

Joan Ganz Cooney didn't get the nickname "Guts" for nothing. In college she may have switched her major to education because "it was something that girls of my generation did," but she was never going to follow the script of staying put to marry young and well. Dismissing the warning that she'd never be more than a "little fish in a big pond," Joan set off to New York City to chase a career in the communications industry. A young idealist deeply influenced by the civil rights and Catholic social justice movements, Joan saw media as a means for instigating change. Her initial gig—writing soap opera summaries—made her feel like a very small fish, but Joan had a knack for hustling and networking her way to the next big opportunity. After cutting her teeth as a show publicist, she convinced a new public network to hire her as a producer. Three years later, a 1966 dinner-party conversation with a prominent philanthropist set her on the path to catalyzing a radical innovation in early childhood education for all: TV programs designed to teach.

The nonprofit Carnegie Corporation tapped Joan to investigate if the small screen could provide meaningful lessons to preschoolers. She saw huge potential, especially for underprivileged kids. Her landmark report laid the framework for the show that would become *Sesame Street*. When the funders decided to recruit a big-name executive to make that show a reality, Joan declined the offer of being #2, instead securing the top spot as one of the first female TV execs. *Sesame Street* first aired in 1969 to instant public and parental acclaim. Now, more than 4,000 alphabet-sponsored episodes and 170 Emmys later, the show remains a childhood staple and educational entertainment empire, with Big Bird and his friends adapted for broadcasts in 140 countries with an audience of more than 100 million. Meanwhile, "Saint Joan of Television" is using her "*Street*" smarts and her namesake nonprofit to spur the next wave of innovation in children's education and media.

> "
>
> # How do you know I won't be a big fish in a big pond?
>
> "

JOAN GANZ COONEY
SESAME STREET COCREATOR

Sally Ride

1951–2012

SPACE INSTITUTE DIRECTOR • 1ST US WOMAN IN SPACE •
ALL-STAR SCIENCE COMMUNICATOR

Sally Ride's 1983 blastoff in the space shuttle *Challenger* established her as the ultimate barrier-breaking inspiration to women around the world. The lead-up to her historic launch bore hints of how strong the barriers in the industry had been. A prior training program for female astronauts (underwritten by pioneering pilot Jacqueline Cochran) had been deemed a failure by NASA. Twenty years later, the space agency's male engineers fretted about accommodating what they assumed to be Sally's needs, designing a makeup kit for zero gravity and provisioning her with no fewer than 100 tampons for the 6-day flight. During the pre-mission publicity tour, journalists showed no interest in the robotic arm she'd be operating or satellites she'd be deploying. Instead, they asked if she was prone to crying under pressure and how space might affect her reproductive organs. Sally handled it with stellar poise. She'd been selected from among 8,000 applicants for NASA's astronaut class of 1978—the first to officially recruit a pool beyond male engineers and military pilots. Sally, a Stanford doctoral candidate in physics who had once chased a pro tennis career, was one of six women who got the nod. Her scientific background and athletic prowess helped her excel in training, eventually landing her the historic call-up to be the first US woman and youngest American in space. Sally would go on to many more frontier-pushing firsts, from serving as the founding director of NASA's Office of Exploration to being the first woman to have a Navy research ship named after her.

When the astrophysics prof later recalled her two spaceflights, it was the sheer pleasure that stuck with her. Describing her missions as the most fun she'd ever had, Sally dedicated herself to communicating that magic of discovery to the next generation, especially girls. Besides authoring seven children's books that offer awe-inspiring, astronaut's-eye views of our solar system and home planet, she founded Sally Ride Science to promote equal access to STEM education. She'd be thrilled to know that the gender ratio for incoming astronaut classes is now a solid 50/50.

There's something magical about pushing back the frontiers of knowledge.

SALLY RIDE
ASTRONAUT

Amanda Nguyen

born 1991

DAUGHTER OF VIETNAMESE REFUGEES • ADVOCATE FOR SURVIVORS • SOCIAL ENTREPRENEUR

In October 2016, 25-year-old Amanda Nguyen saw the bill she'd written and advocated for signed into federal law. The Sexual Assault Survivor Bill of Rights was one of only 21 pieces of legislation to have been passed unanimously through both houses of the US Congress. Its origin story was Amanda's own survivor's story. She was assaulted while attending Harvard and had a rape kit performed, but decided not to press charges until she was ready to face the trial. The police told her she had 15 years to bring her case, but as it turned out, the lynchpin evidence from her 6-hour forensic examination wouldn't last nearly that long. State law dictated that her kit would only be held six months. Soon she found that some states would destroy kits in as little as 30 days if legal proceedings weren't initiated. Amanda had just completed a NASA internship and was training to become an astronaut when she decided it was time to organize her fellow survivors to address the gaps in law that made navigating the criminal justice system so traumatic. Amanda founded Rise in 2014, leading the all-volunteer organization in her spare time while she worked for the State Department. Rise began championing legislation that would codify the civil rights of assault victims, ensuring evidence would be safeguarded, accessible, and free of charge to collect.

Massachusetts was the first target. When Amanda heard their bill was unlikely to pass in the House, she mobilized her Rise team to lobby representatives. After 14 straight hours of face-to-face meetings, they'd taken the legislation from no-go to shoo-in. Amanda's "Risers" have applied that lesson about the power of showing up and speaking from experience to get 20+ laws on the books, protecting more than 72 million people. Effecting landmark legislation in her own country might seem like the ultimate victory, but for Amanda, it's just the start. With the Nobel Peace Prize nominee at the helm full-time, Rise is backing similar bills in all 50 states and launching a global campaign to help victims from countries around the world become authors of their own civil rights.

I could accept the injustice
or rewrite the law. And so
I rewrote it.

AMANDA NGUYEN
CIVIL RIGHTS STARTUP FOUNDER

BRAVELY

"It's time to stop pursuing perfection
and start chasing bravery instead."

RESHMA SAUJANI
STEM NONPROFIT FOUNDER

Harriet Tubman

between 1819 and 1823–1913

UNDERGROUND RAILROAD CONDUCTOR • UNION SCOUT •
FUTURE FACE OF THE $20 BILL

Americans rightfully rank Harriet Tubman among the nation's all-time greatest heroes. An escaped slave who fought to secure freedom for others, she was an intrepid abolitionist torchbearer and later a revered civil rights icon. Born into bondage in Maryland, she was hired out for hard labor by the age of five. In 1849, Harriet fled with two of her brothers, who turned back in fear while she trekked on to the free Commonwealth of Pennsylvania. Over the course of a decade, she repeatedly put her life and liberty on the line to make risky return trips south. As the bounty on her head swelled to a whopping $40K, she guided 19 successful trips on the Underground Railroad, never losing a "passenger" along the way. During the Civil War, Harriet faithfully served as a scout, nurse, and cook for the Union, all while selling pies and root beer to supplement her meager Army wages. She directed the Combahee River Raid that liberated more than 700 slaves, making her the first woman in US history to lead an armed assault in enemy territory. It may have taken her 34 years to receive a veteran's pension, but she was buried with full military honors and given the nod as the namesake for the US Maritime Commission's first Liberty Ship.

While Harriet's legend lives on, her words sadly do not. She didn't learn to write until late in life. Though she gave many speeches as a celebrated public figure—including stumping for women's suffrage—they were not recorded. What traces we have of her voice are filtered through biographers. An abolitionist admirer cited "I can't die but once" as Harriet's emboldening personal motto. Whether or not she said it, she certainly lived those words. When the woman who had always given all she could did die at a surprisingly ripe old age, it was on the property she donated to be used as a care home for poor and elderly African Americans.

I can't die but once.

HARRIET TUBMAN
FREEDOM FIGHTER

Ida Lewis

1842–1911

Ida Lewis made her first sea rescue at age 12, her last when she was 63. In her most widely publicized venture, she narrowly rescued two soldiers whose sailboat had capsized during a sudden March snowstorm, jumping into her rowboat before she even had the chance to put her shoes on. During Ida's 50 years as a lighthouse keeper, she saved at least 18 people (plus a sheep) from drowning. Braving the Atlantic came naturally to Ida. Born in the bustling harbor and fort post of Newport, Rhode Island—an eventual resort hot spot for the Gilded Age elite—she moved to the outcrop of Lime Rock when her father was tapped to run its lighthouse. As a young teen, her daily commutes to deliver her siblings to school sculpted her into a skilled boater and agile swimmer. When her father suffered a stroke in 1857, she and her mother assumed daily maintenance of the lighthouse. Ida was only granted the official keeper title decades later in 1879, after the death of both her parents, but she ultimately became the US's highest paid keeper.

During her lifetime, Ida's immense courage made her a bona fide national celeb. She wowed on the cover of *Harper's*, inspired a popular waltz, and became the first woman to receive the US Coast Guard's Gold Lifesaving Medal. In her hometown, local vendors sold Ida Lewis hats and scarves while residents hosted a parade in her honor, giving her an extravagantly impractical boat of ornately carved mahogany, complete with velvet cushions and gold-plated oarlocks. She was visited by President Ulysses S. Grant, regularly held up as a paragon of feminine strength by Elizabeth Cady Stanton, accosted with numerous marriage proposals, and had her tiny island besieged by thousands of fans. Through it all, Ida remained steadfast in her duties and humble in her outlook. She's still a local legend in Newport, where the island and lighthouse she lived in until her death now bear her name . . . as does the first road named after a woman in Arlington National Cemetery.

"If there were some people out there who needed help, I would get into my boat and go to them even if I knew I couldn't get back. Wouldn't you?"

IDA LEWIS
LIGHTHOUSE KEEPER

Virginia Hall

1906–1982

SOCIALITE TURNED SPY • AMPUTEE WITH A NEW LEASE
ON LIFE • TRAILBLAZING CIA OPERATIVE

She may have been born into a Baltimore banking dynasty, but Virginia Hall never sought a pampered life. As an accomplished language student she dreamed of joining the Foreign Service, but the odds were stacked against her: only 6 of 1,500 staffers were women. When Virginia lost half her leg after an overseas hunting accident, another excuse emerged to deny her applications: amputees were barred from diplomatic service. With the outbreak of World War II, Virginia gave up. She resigned her post as a clerk with the US Consulate in Turkey and went to the front lines to drive ambulances for the French Army during the 1940 Nazi invasion. When France fell, she headed to the UK to volunteer with the British. On the way, she had a chance encounter with an intelligence officer. He became convinced that Winston Churchill's newly minted secret service for undercover warfare could use someone with Virginia's valor, grit, and resourcefulness. The first female agent dispatched from London, she posed as a *New York Post* reporter operating behind enemy lines. Virginia's unmatched success at recruiting informants, eluding the Gestapo, and engineering sensational jailbreaks convinced the Allies to enlist more women for the cause.

Though her sex initially helped Virginia go under the radar, the Gestapo eventually wised up and issued a Wanted poster identifying the "Lady with the Limp" as the "enemy's most dangerous spy." The British decommissioned her following a near capture, so she signed on to go undercover for the US instead, applying makeup and even filing down her teeth to assume the guise of an aging French milkmaid. She built up a network of 1,500 resistance fighters, organizing and commanding guerrilla attacks that won back strategic targets and paved the way for victory. Virginia returned home as the war's most highly decorated female civilian, but kept her exploits a secret for the rest of her life. Though underappreciated during her ensuing career with the fledgling CIA, Virginia is now lauded among the agency's finest. They've named a training facility in her honor, shared her epic feats beyond the intelligence community, and acknowledged they still consult her playbook when planning missions.

My neck is my own. If I am willing to get a crick in it, I think that's my prerogative.

VIRGINIA HALL
UNDERCOVER AGENT

Jody Williams

born 1950

INTERNATIONAL AID WORKER • SOCIAL JUSTICE PROF •
NOBEL LAUREATE REDEFINING PEACE

Jody Williams was a newly minted grad of international politics when her work with Central American aid organizations gave her a startling hands-on lesson. Posted in civil war–torn El Salvador, she had the grim job of providing artificial limbs to children who lost arms and legs to land mines. This experience made her realize what a grave threat the concealed explosive devices posed, not only to combatants, but entire civilian populations. Worst of all, the menace of these weapons remained long after the fighting stopped. In 1991, Jody was invited by two NGOs—a veterans' group and a medical relief organization—to investigate the possibilities for forging an international coalition to address the 100 million land mines perilously dotted around the globe. As the founding coordinator of the International Campaign to Ban Landmines she grew the organization exponentially, enlisting 1,300 groups in 95 countries to sign on as supporters, as well as celebrity advocates like Princess Diana. In just six years, Jody generated enough political momentum and community backing to broker an unprecedented diplomatic achievement: a Mine Ban Treaty that's been ratified by 130 countries and counting, virtually eliminating the new use, trade, and production of land mines. The feat won Jody the 1997 Nobel Peace Prize, but she didn't rest on her laureate. Besides addressing the explosives still buried in 61 countries that affect thousands of victims each year, she continues to monitor the treaty's implementation, ensuring that signatories honor their commitments.

Today, the endowed chair of social work at the University of Houston is expanding her mission to spread a "realistic" vision for world peace. In 2006, she teamed with her sister laureates to launch the Nobel Women's Initiative. They're using their clout to back projects that contribute locally or globally to justice and equality. The group is part of Jody's effort to reframe how we think about peace—not as a rainbow or dove or any other abstract utopian ideal, but as a daily human responsibility to work toward environmental justice, sustainable development, and the guarantee of a dignified life for all.

66

Peace is not a rainbow and a dove. It is hard work every single day to try and reshape our understanding of the world.

99

JODY WILLIAMS
PEACE ACTIVIST

Simone Biles

born 1997

MOVE INVENTOR & NAMESAKE • MOST DECORATED GYMNAST IN US HISTORY • INSPIRING SURVIVOR

The gravity-defying Simone Biles has won more world medals than any gymnast on Earth. This unshakable, record-breaking dominance has led many to dub her the GOAT in her sport. Yet remarkably, this highflier's passion was something she tumbled upon by chance. When addiction issues left Simone's single mother unable to care for her and her siblings, they were adopted by their grandparents in Texas. Not long after, a rainy-day field trip led her to a gymnastics studio. The 6-year-old's enthusiasm for mimicking the athletes' moves so impressed the coach that he sent a letter encouraging the energetic kid to enroll. The budding phenom quickly stood out as a serious and charismatic competitor, known for cracking crowd-stealing smiles and cheering on teammates. Simone's stunning debut on the senior circuit saw her top the podium at both the national and world championships. Her career vaulted to new heights when she emerged three years later as a superstar of the 2016 Rio Olympics, where she tied the record for most medals won by a gymnast in a single year—five, including four Golds! She sealed the all-around title with a statement-making margin of 2.1 points—a larger gap than those from the previous nine Olympics combined. Currently in her 20s, the bold 4'8" risk-taker is continuing to push the limits of her sport, adding to her historic title count while landing never-before-attempted moves, like a triple-twisting double somersault. She now has four moves officially named after her that rank among the most difficult skills ever performed.

Simone's physical and mental strength on the mats have long been admired. These days, she's also earning props for her personal courage. Since coming forward as one of 300 survivors of sexual abuse perpetrated by the now imprisoned US national team doctor, Simone has bravely shared the struggles that nearly sank her aspirations. Now the woman dubbed one of *Time*'s most influential people is using her sway to ensure young athletes can fearlessly and safely focus on what's most important: pursuing their own audacious goals and dreams.

66

I'd rather regret the risks
that didn't work out than
the chances I didn't take.

99

SIMONE BILES
GYMNAST

CANDIDLY

"We must be able to separate the trivia of today from the enduring realities of the long tomorrows. Having recognized and defined our values, we must defend them without fear and without apology."

RACHEL CARSON
CONSERVATIONIST

Ida B. Wells

1862–1931

CIVIL & WOMEN'S RIGHTS LEADER • NEWSPAPER EDITOR & PUBLISHER • COURAGEOUS TRUTH-TELLER

Ida B. Wells was born in Mississippi during the Civil War to a slave couple who became political leaders during Reconstruction. She set her maverick course early, getting expelled from the college her father helped found for picking a fight with its president. In 1882, Ida was forcibly removed from a train for trying to claim the seat she'd purchased with a first-class ticket. Afterward, the young teacher began devoting her uncompromising voice to commenting on race issues. Initially publishing articles under the pseudonym "Iola," she soon became a publisher in her own right as the co-owner of the Memphis *Free Speech and Headlight.* When a friend was lynched in 1892, Ida pursued the weighty subject for her first major in-depth investigation, treading on risky territory to research 700 lynching cases across the South. Armed with a pistol in case her questions backfired, she visited crime scenes, scrutinized photos and local press accounts, and conducted eyewitness interviews. Her dangerously candid reports on the dishonorable motivations behind what were billed as "just killings" made her a target for retaliation. Ida's press and offices were destroyed, and the mounting barrage of threats forced her to move north.

Ida wouldn't, however, be silenced. A pioneer of data journalism, she was the first to compile national lynching stats, circulating them in a chastening pamphlet called "The Red Record" and giving lectures around the world to educate people on the scale of the problem. Ida also joined with others to promote equal rights. Besides being a founding member of the NAACP, she created Chicago's Alpha Suffrage Club, which was instrumental in winning Illinois women the vote in 1913. That same year, she was invited to attend the first mass suffragist parade in the nation's capital. True to her nature, the rebel with a cause refused to obey the organizers' request for black women to keep to the back of the procession, joining the Chicago contingent midway through to march into history on her own terms.

The way to right wrongs is to turn the light of truth upon them.

99

IDA B. WELLS
INVESTIGATIVE JOURNALIST

Frances Perkins

1880–1965

INDUSTRIAL RELATIONS PROF • 1ST FEMALE US CABINET MEMBER • "ARCHITECT OF THE NEW DEAL"

Frances Perkins had long been the New York governor's top labor adviser when he appointed her to be the state's industrial commissioner in 1929. She sealed her acceptance with a solemn pledge, promising to "use what brains I have to meet problems with intelligence and courage" and share "the whole truth so far as I can speak it." A winning combination of highly educated and highly motivated, Frances was bent on bettering the lives of working people with daring new policies sparked by data-rich research. It was a calling she came upon in college after touring nearby mills at the behest of her industrial history professor. Shocked by the long hours and poor conditions endured by child and women workers, the physics major decided to retrain. She earned another BS and grad degree in sociology and economics while volunteering with immigrants at Jane Addams's Hull House in Chicago. After moving to New York, Frances spearheaded reports on childhood malnutrition and became the local leader for her idol Florence Kelly's Consumer League, a group lobbying for workers' rights. After personally witnessing girls jump to their deaths during the Triangle Shirtwaist factory fire that claimed 146 lives, she became a go-to expert witness and investigator for the committee tasked with redressing the tragedy, ushering in a nation-leading package of workplace health and safety regulations.

Frances's political profile continued to rise until, in 1933, during the leanest days of the Great Depression, newly elected President Franklin D. Roosevelt asked her to be his labor secretary. She informed him that she would only take the post if he'd agree to back her entire program of bold reforms. Of her proposals—including mass public employment through major infrastructure projects, a ban on child labor, nationalized unemployment insurance and pensions, a standardized minimum wage, and a 40-hour workweek—only one (universal health insurance) did not come to pass. In fact, Frances's brainchildren, like the Civilian Conservation Corps and Social Security, became hallmarks of FDR's New Deal. To this day, the longest-serving US secretary of labor and ever-alert reformer remains a role model for turning disquiet into decisive action.

" A healthy discontent keeps us alert to the changing needs of our time. "

FRANCES PERKINS
LABOR SECRETARY

Esther "Eppie" Lederer

1918–2002

INTUITIVE ADVISER • WORLD'S MOST WIDELY SYNDICATED COLUMNIST • FOREMOTHER OF SOCIAL FRANKNESS

In 1955, with no previous experience in journalism, Eppie Lederer handily won a contest to replace the original author of the "Ask Ann Landers" column in the *Chicago Sun-Times*. With her frank wit and distinctly modern moral sensibility, Eppie made Ann the most widely read advice-giver of all time, appearing in 1,200 newspapers for a global audience of 90 million. Operating entirely via mail, Eppie received as many as 2,000 letters a day, written by everyone from lovesick teens to perplexed parents. She handpicked features that would call attention to thorny and timely topics—like divorce, depression, bereavement, teen pregnancy, addiction, racism, and AIDS—and pioneered the practice of bringing in experts when an issue fell outside her domain. Though some of Ann's opinions would inevitably change over the course of her 47-year career, the trademark tone of her commonsense counsel, dished up with a dash of humor, remained a constant. A regular dealer in puns and soon-to-be aphorisms, she admonished a man considering an affair in her very first column, using the line "Time wounds all heels." Her personal mottoes—like "Wake up and smell the coffee"—became national catchphrases.

Beyond her winning one-liners, Eppie's charm was her candor about her own very human problems and failings. For one, her main professional rival, "Dear Abby's" Abigail van Buren, was in fact her twin sister. Born 17 minutes apart to Jewish immigrant parents in Iowa, they were so close they attended the same college, dropping out together to plan their double wedding. When the two became figureheads of competing advice dynasties, it caused a family feud that took five years to resolve. Eppie also announced the end of her 36-year marriage in a 1975 column, confiding to readers: "The lady with all the answers doesn't know the answer to this one." If her advice met with well-founded criticism, she'd print the rebuttals and sentence herself to "40 lashes with a wet noodle." Often dubbed "America's mother," Eppie was the first journalist to win a Lasker Award—a nod to her far-reaching service to public health and wellness.

"

The naked truth is always better than the best-dressed lie.

"

ANN LANDERS
ADVICE COLUMNIST

Ruth Bader Ginsburg

1933–2020

LAW PROFESSOR & PROMINENT LITIGATOR • VISIONARY DISSENTER • POP CULTURE PHENOM

In 1993, Ruth Bader Ginsburg was confirmed in a near-unanimous Senate vote as the second woman appointed to the US Supreme Court. Ruth had made a name for herself as a leading gender discrimination litigator in the 1970s, bringing six cases all the way to the highest court in the land and winning all but one. As the founding counsel for the ACLU's Women's Rights Project, she sagely worked with both male and female plaintiffs to show how discriminatory policies hinder both sexes. She'd triumphed over the bias she'd met within her own career—like receiving zero job offers from firms despite graduating #1 in her class—to become Columbia Law's first female tenured faculty member. Yet she didn't hesitate for a second to swap her professor's podium or lawyer's table for a judge's bench when the opportunity arose in 1980.

During her 27-year tenure on the nation's highest bench, the petite octogenarian became a living legend for her frank and outsize opinions. In 2013, an NYU law student cleverly dubbed her "The Notorious RBG" after late rapper The Notorious BIG (with whom, Ruth graciously noted, she shared much in common, like hailing from Brooklyn). It didn't take long for the moniker to go viral. Besides featuring on flashy neon apparel and accessories, RBG has been the subject of books, films, and even a popular comic opera celebrating her unexpected friendship with the late conservative justice Antonin Scalia. Famous for wearing lace collars interwoven with symbolism over her sober judicial robes and for refusing to step down even after four bouts of cancer, Ruth remains a pop culture icon for the power of opposition. A firm believer that "dissents speak to a future age," she made as many waves with her incisive minority opinions—some of which prompted corrective legislation—as she did with her precedent-setting majority decisions. A trailblazer even in death, the deceased justice became the first woman to lie in state at the US Capitol.

"

If you're going to change things, you have to be with the people who hold the levers.

RUTH BADER GINSBURG
SUPREME COURT JUSTICE

Janet Mock

born 1983

#GIRLSLIKEUS ADVOCATE • EDITOR & PRODUCER • CULTURE-SHIFTING CONTENT MOGUL

Janet Mock knew she was a girl in a boy's body, but that was a tough thing to articulate while growing up in a broken, low-income family with a father who kept trying to "fix her." It wasn't until the 12-year-old rejoined her mother in her native Hawaii—where there's traditionally been a more fluid sense of gender identity, including the word *māhū* for a third—that she was able to begin exploring and claiming her identity. A community of friends and mentors helped her transition. When she went to study journalism in New York, 5,000 miles from her hometown, Janet began "passing" as a woman. But five years into her life as an editor at *People* magazine Janet still felt like she was hiding. Haunted by harrowing stats that show trans people are among society's most vulnerable demographics—susceptible to homelessness, unemployment, violence, and suicide—she felt compelled to share her hopeful story of weathering the storm and flourishing.

Janet's 2014 memoir *Redefining Realness* was a literary landmark—the first mainstream autobiographical account of a young transgender person's journey. In it, she offers heartening and gut-wrenching insights into the extremes that defined her coming of age, from being a popular honors student to not only suffering sexual abuse but feeling like she—as a "sissy"—deserved it. Her genius for storytelling caught the eye of small-screen powerhouse Ryan Murphy, who saw in Janet a mogul in the making. He invited her to join his writing team for *Pose*, making her one of the first trans women of color behind the camera. Now, the budding writer-director-producer is poised to open a world of storytelling with a historic Netflix deal that will give her license to create revolutionary programming—including an adaptation of her memoir. Cast in bronze as one of the first 10 women featured in New York City's Statues for Equality project, Janet boldly stands as the embodiment of living your truth.

"Those parts of yourself that you desperately want to hide and destroy will gain power over you. The best thing to do is face and own them."

JANET MOCK
WRITER-DIRECTOR

COMPASSIONATELY

"The good that we secure for ourselves is precarious and uncertain, is floating in mid-air, until it is secured for all of us."

JANE ADDAMS
SOCIAL REFORMER

Sarah Winnemucca

1844–1891

AUTHOR & LECTURER • 1ST NATIVE AMERICAN TO PEN A BOOK ON HER PEOPLE • CULTURAL TRANSLATOR

Sarah Winnemucca was the daughter of a Numa chief, born during a period of US territorial expansion. As settlers migrated west, they encroached on the land of Sarah's people—known by pioneers as the Northern Paiutes—that spanned present-day Nevada and Oregon. While her father kept a wary distance from the new arrivals, her grandfather greeted them as brothers, encouraging his granddaughters to learn their language and customs. Sarah realized that bad or good, they were there to stay. She decided to assume the role of translator and ambassador for her tribe. By the time she was 14, the young linguist had mastered five languages, including English, Spanish, and three Indian dialects.

In the 1870s, the Paiutes were forced onto reservations. Having always lived as hunters and gatherers, they were now expected, with few resources and no training, to exist as self-sustaining farm communities. With many of her people facing starvation, Sarah sought aid from a nearby military camp. She managed to secure supplies and was hired as an interpreter, eventually serving as a messenger, scout, and translator during the 1878 Bannock War. She thought her exemplary service and tribe's compliance would secure them better treatment. Instead, they were marched hundreds of miles to a new reservation. Outraged, Sarah led an envoy to Washington, DC to plead her people's case. Her in-person appeals to the president, secretary of the interior, and military leaders exacted many promises, none of which were kept. So she turned to the public. In 1883 she wrote *Life Among the Piutes*, the first published narrative in English written by a Native American woman. Besides documenting the plight of her people, the book pays tribute to tribal customs, including treating everyone with hospitality and kindness regardless of their social standing. Sarah's well-received writings and nearly 300 lectures made her a much-lauded orator. Unfortunately, they didn't yield a single policy change. Those she had tried so fiercely yet fruitlessly to advocate for had come to distrust her. Nevertheless, she kept striving to help, founding a reservation school as the last act in her tireless struggle to bridge cultures and foster understanding.

"

Be kind to both bad
and good, for you don't
know your own heart.

"

SARAH WINNEMUCCA
INDIGENOUS RIGHTS ACTIVIST

Eleanor Roosevelt

1884–1962

ADVOCATE & AUTHOR • PROTOTYPE OF
THE MODERN FIRST LADY • GLOBAL DIPLOMAT

Decades after Eleanor Roosevelt left Washington, DC as the longest-serving first lady, she remains one of the most admired and quoted people in the world. Even widely circulated misattributions speak to her status as a beacon of wisdom, an international icon of tremendous personal courage and boundless compassion. Eleanor was born into a life of great privilege, though being a New York society girl whose uncle was President Theodore Roosevelt didn't shield her from shyness, awkwardness, or the grief of losing both her parents and younger brother. The headmistress of her boarding school took a special interest in Eleanor, drawing the heartsick student out of her shell to emerge as the confident, independent thinker she would ultimately become in the White House. Serving through some of the most pivotal moments in US history, spanning the Great Depression to World War II, she transformed the role of president's wife from polite, fashionable hostess to vocal advocate for social issues, including women's, workers', and civil rights. When her husband Franklin lost his ability to walk, Eleanor became his legs and ears, traveling the nation to better understand the needs of the people. In each of the 12 years of his administration, she received 175,000 letters and delivered 75 speeches. By the end of her prolific career, she had inspired fellow citizens with 27 books, 233 radio shows, 580 articles, and 8,000+ installments of her syndicated column. Filled with poignant personal anecdotes and influential editorials, "My Day" ran six days a week from 1936 until her death in 1962.

The authorship cred Eleanor was most proud of was an international collaboration. After WWII, she was appointed as US delegate to the General Assembly of the newly formed United Nations, where she chaired the committee that created its foundational "Declaration of Human Rights." She spent the rest of her life trying to bring about that vision for a peaceful global order based on freedom, respect, and opportunity for all. Her unflagging advocacy saw her eulogized with a title that's stuck: "First Lady to the World."

> **"**
>
> Our mutual devotion to our own land must never blind us to the good of all lands and all peoples.
>
> **"**

ELEANOR ROOSEVELT
HUMANITARIAN

Marian Wright Edelman

born 1939

LAWYER • BEST-SELLING AUTHOR • NONPROFIT FOUNDER & JUSTICE CRUSADER

In 2018, Marian Wright Edelman stepped down as president of the Children's Defense Fund. She had founded the nonprofit agency more than 40 years earlier in 1973, building it into the country's leading advocacy organization for children and families. Under her watch, the CDF did everything from pushing for expanded public health care coverage and juvenile justice reform to running no-cost summer academic enrichment programs and conducting critical research into child welfare. Many a Head Start program around the nation is named in Marian's honor, a nod to how instrumental she was in securing funding for the initiative to help level the playing field in early childhood education. Though the reach of Marian's mission has extended into many complex policy areas, the underlying sentiment has remained a constant: "I want for other people's children what I want for my own children."

Marian once dreamed of a very different sort of career. Her sophomore year at Spelman College, she'd earned a scholarship to study abroad in Paris and Geneva. After growing up under segregation in South Carolina, attending integrated classes in Europe made Marian feel liberated. She fell in love with Russian literature and wanted to become a scholar. But when she returned home, she found a country engulfed in the struggle over civil rights. Marian gave up her personal aspiration to throw herself into the ranks of the movement fighting for everyone to have that same sense of freedom and possibility. When her friends' arrest at a sit-in protest made her realize there were only three lawyers in Mississippi working on civil rights cases, Marian enrolled in Yale Law, later becoming the first black woman admitted to the Mississippi bar. She directed the state's NAACP Legal Defense and Educational Fund before moving to Washington, DC in 1968 to serve as counsel for Dr. Martin Luther King Jr.'s Poor People's Campaign. Inspired by his efforts, Marian dedicated the rest of her professional life to improving the prospects of disadvantaged Americans. Her "compassionate action" has been recognized with a MacArthur Genius Award, Presidential Medal of Freedom, and more than 100 honorary degrees.

"It's time for greatness—not for greed. It's time for idealism—not ideology. It's time not just for compassionate words, but compassionate action."

MARIAN WRIGHT EDELMAN
CHILDREN'S RIGHTS ADVOCATE

Jacqueline Novogratz

born 1961

BANKER • IMPACT-INVESTING PIONEER •
COMPASSIONATE NONCONFORMIST

At six years old, Jacqueline Novogratz took to heart the age-old axiom "to whom much is given, much is expected" instilled by her first-grade teacher Sister Mary Theophane. This adage stirred her desire to change the world. In her first job out of college, Jacqueline got the chance to see a lot of it. Working for the credit audit division of a major bank, she traveled extensively to assess the quality of their loans. When a trip to Brazil confronted her with the huge gulf between rich and poor, she ventured to ask her manager if they could do more for those at the bottom of the pyramid. The answer was a definitive "no," defended with familiar reasons of why it would be too risky and costly. Jacqueline's response was to quit her job on Wall Street and imagine a new kind of investing, one that would measure results in terms of social impact.

When the 20-something idealist opted to begin her good works in Africa, she quickly realized that people there neither wanted nor needed saving. Giving up the charitable mindset that reinforces the gap between rich and poor, Jacqueline instead listened keenly. In 1986, she partnered with Kigali women to set up a thriving local bakery operated by formerly ostracized residents and created the country's first microfinance institution run by and for Rwandans. After heading back to the US for her MBA, Jacqueline made her next big move in 2001, launching Acumen, a "nonprofit venture capital fund for the poor." Since then, the first-of-its-kind organization has invested $110 million to finance more than 100 social enterprises, from Colombia to Uganda. Backing companies and entrepreneurs whose innovations in education, health care, sanitation, energy, and agriculture have improved the lives of more than 200 million people, Jacqueline's "patient capital" has reached places that markets and government aid don't touch. Recently named among the "World's Greatest Living Business Minds," the impact investor remains on the front lines of a moral revolution in business and a business revolution in philanthropy.

> "Your job is not to be perfect. Your job is only to be human."

JACQUELINE NOVOGRATZ
SOCIAL ENTREPRENEUR

Elisabeth Keller

born 1958

NURSE-MIDWIFE • ORGANIC FARM PRESIDENT • VENTURE INVESTOR & PHILANTHROPIST

Elisabeth Keller's childhood home was an 1836 plantation house on a 3,000-acre Louisiana farming estate. Inglewood had been in her family and managed by various relatives since 1926. When Elisabeth took over after an early career in public health, it was a conventional commodity crop operation planted with cotton, corn, and soybeans. The onetime nurse and divinity student decided to do something unconventional. In 2007, she began transitioning her family's profitable holdings to more sustainable agricultural practices. It was a tough row to hoe. Though the organic movement had been around since the 1960s and is one of the fastest-growing sectors of the food industry, the Deep South had been slow to adopt the trend. When Elisabeth sought advice from other farmers, they assured her that going without chemical insecticides would never fly in the notoriously hot, humid, pest-ridden climes of Central Louisiana. Still, if Inglewood could germinate a wider movement in her home state, she knew it was worth the risk. By the time they'd knuckled down and experimented to convert 1,000 acres to raising organic vegetables, grains, pecans, and livestock in 2012, theirs was only the seventh certified farm in all of Louisiana. By far the state's largest organic operation, Elisabeth's model has indeed borne fruit—the number of organic producers tripled within four years and continues to rise.

Her example is sending out shoots in other ways, too. A longtime philanthropist, Elisabeth is invested in growing her community alongside her okra, rojo peppers, and turnip greens. In fact, Inglewood has become a model "organic hot spot," boosting the local economy with a fresh crop of farm-to-table restaurants and six artisan-empowering farmers' markets in rural towns. Elisabeth's also keen to ensure the benefits of their life-giving efforts aren't limited to a select few. Partnering with a regional food bank, she set up 75 school and community gardens that have gotten thousands of kids and residents to take up a trowel. It's her way of cultivating not only healthy lifestyles but compassionate values—like kindness to each other and the Earth.

"

What do I want to grow that will be sustaining and life-giving to the community, the world, the planet?

"

ELISABETH KELLER
ORGANIC FARMER

CREATIVELY

"I wonder if I'm a raving lunatic for trying
to make these things."

GEORGIA O'KEEFFE
PAINTER

Florence Price

1887–1953

STAR PIANIST & ORGANIST • CLASSICAL & POP MUSIC WRITER •
LONG-FORGOTTEN VIRTUOSO

In 2009, a couple was getting ready to renovate a dilapidated house on the outskirts of Chicago when they uncovered a missing piece of US musical heritage—30 dusty boxes filled with papers and lost scores written by composer Florence Price. They were tucked away in a dry corner of what turned out to be her long-abandoned summer home. Though celebrated during her lifetime, Florence died with most of her music unheard and quickly faded from public memory. The first noted black female composer, she studied with her music teacher mother in their Little Rock, Arkansas, home before earning a spot at the prestigious New England Conservatory. She so excelled as a student that she was singled out for private lessons with the school's president. It wasn't until Florence moved to Chicago with her family in 1927 that she began to compose music in earnest. Left a single parent after an acrimonious divorce, she made ends meet by writing radio jingles and silent film soundtracks. But it was her debut symphony that made ears prick up, scoring a 1932 Wanamaker Foundation Award and landing on the Chicago Symphony's program for the following year—the first time a major orchestra had performed work by an African American woman.

Luminous yet accessible, Florence's music artfully blended classical European elements with the styles and rhythms of African American blues and folk traditions. Her creative ambition was to forge distinctively American music with a melting pot of influences, just like the nation itself. She wrote symphonies and concertos, set the work of poets to music, and orchestrated thrilling choral pieces. But she was best known for her widely performed arrangements of spirituals. The incomparable contralto Marian Anderson even chose Florence's rendition of "My Soul's Been Anchored in De Lord" as the finale for her most famous concert—co-organized with Eleanor Roosevelt in 1939 on the steps of the Lincoln Memorial. Today, revived by the recovery of her unpublished masterpieces, Florence is once again getting a listen . . . including a 2019 world premiere of her lost Fourth Symphony by the Fort Smith Symphony in her native Arkansas.

> "
> There is always an ideal toward which we strive, and ideals, as you know, are elusive.... They escape our human hands, but lead us on, and I trust upward.
> "

FLORENCE PRICE
COMPOSER

Rita Moreno

born 1931

SINGER & DANCER • 1ST LATINA TO ACHIEVE EGOT STATUS •
ARDENT ARTS ADVOCATE

When Rita Moreno was five years old, she left behind her hometown on the edge of the Puerto Rican rain forest and sailed with her seamstress mother to New York City. It was a storm-tossed journey, but when the Statue of Liberty finally came into view, Rita took it as a good omen. After all, how bad could this place be if there was a woman in charge? Her mother worked in a sweatshop so the talented youngster could take dance classes, using any spare time to sew costumes for Rita's performances around their Brooklyn barrio. When her daughter was scouted by Hollywood agents at 13, it looked like the sacrifices they'd made to go to the land of opportunity had paid off. MGM Studios signed Rita to a 7-year contract, but her stint there was full of typecasting into any nonwhite role, whether Polynesian, Egyptian, Native American, or Burmese. Often playing the spurned lover, she was obliged to deliver lines like, "Why you no love Ula no more?"

In 1961, Rita had a breakthrough moment, professionally and personally. She was tapped to play tough girl Anita in the hit film musical *West Side Story*. Her brilliant performance earned her an Oscar and Golden Globe (she'd nab the other three major entertainment awards—an Emmy, Grammy, and Tony—by the time she was 45). It also gave her a lesson in self-respect. She decided to never again take a role unless it was artful and allowed her to be "Hispanic with dignity." Rita's firm stance temporarily halted her film career and forced her toward the stage and small screen, where she wowed in a Broadway rendition of *The Ritz* and won new fans in the original cast of the PBS kids series *The Electric Company*. Today, the much celebrated Walk-of-Famer regularly stumps for the arts as a soul-nourishing part of personal and societal development. Her most recent screen cred? Executive producer for the Steven Spielberg remake of her beloved *West Side Story* . . . this time with Latinx actors in the leads.

Art is nourishment for the soul; it's a mirror held up to show us who we are and who we can become.

RITA MORENO
ACTOR

Jeanne Gang

born 1964

STUDIO FOUNDER & PROFESSOR IN PRACTICE • ECO-INNOVATOR •
MODERN "RELATIONSHIP BUILDER"

As a kid, Jeanne Gang spent blustery Midwest winters building ice castles in the snow. Little did she imagine that her first high-profile commission as an architect would be to design one of the highest skyscrapers in the region's metropolitan hub—Chicago's 82-story Aqua Tower. The state-of-the-art project not only put her Studio Gang on the map as one of the field's most innovative firms—and gave Jeanne the record for the tallest building designed by a woman—it helped people recognize once again the possibilities of urban architecture to construct sustainable, equitable, and socially engaged communities. Inspired by ecology's focus on the finely balanced networks that underlie thriving habitats, Jeanne thinks of herself first and foremost as a "relationship builder," creating spaces that connect people with their environment and each other. That's a difficult thing to do in the vertical orientation of big cities, but Jeanne gave us the blueprint. For Aqua, she devised a system of offset balconies that encourage residents to interact as if chatting between backyards. Blending style and function, the balconies artfully evoke rippling water while also blocking the Windy City's gusts. Since then, Jeanne has designed high-rises from Amsterdam to Honolulu and has an even-taller 95-story tower in the works on Chicago's Riverfront.

No matter the scale or medium, purpose is the cornerstone of Jeanne's creative process. She courts pleasure and discovery by seeking a fantastic variety of commissions and approaching them all with openness. She's reimagined a forbidding inner-city police station as a trust-rebuilding "polis station" complete with barbershops and basketball courts. She's repurposed a 100-year-old coal-burning power plant into a university health and wellness center, designed sleek boathouses that organically filter runoff, and turned an artificial island into one of the largest urban aquatic nature preserves. Recently dubbed the world's most influential architect by *Time*, Jeanne's latest commissions will leave her inventive mark on iconic sites, including the US Embassy in Brazil, Chicago's O'Hare Airport, and New York City's Natural History Museum.

> **"**
>
> Pleasure and discovery often stem from looking at the world with openness, as if we are seeing it for the first time.
>
> **"**

JEANNE GANG
URBAN ARCHITECT

Alice Wong

born 1974

MEDICAL SOCIOLOGIST • DISABILITY RIGHTS LEADER •
AUTHOR, EDITOR & MEDIA MAKER

While celebrating the 25th anniversary of the Americans with Disabilities Act (ADA), activist Alice Wong rolled into the Oval Office virtually, via a telepresence robot. Controlling its movements remotely and speaking through a webcam, she officially became the White House's first telerobotic visitor, proclaiming herself "half-human, half-robot, 100% proud disabled American." An Indianapolis, Indiana, native with parents from Hong Kong, Alice was born with a spinal cord disorder. A first-generation beneficiary of the ADA, at 18 she was able to apply for Medicaid and gain the independence to pursue her own life and career without relying on her family as caretakers. Since then, the writer and consultant has devoted herself to expanding opportunities for disabled people as writers, makers, and engaged citizens.

After being appointed by cyber-pal President Barack Obama to serve as a member of the National Council on Disability, Alice launched the Disability Visibility Project in 2014. The multimedia endeavor is a vital trove and amplifier of "crip wisdom for the people," with online forums, social media campaigns, oral history videos, print anthologies, and a podcast. Her work has spotlighted everyone from a deaf dancer-choreographer to a stuttering stand-up comedian to a wheelchair-empowered journalist and producer. Besides building supportive communities and raising much-needed awareness, Alice is disrupting stereotypes of the disabled as either disgruntled victims or saintly inspirations by giving more people a platform for sharing their experiences. In most portraits, you'll see her sporting the mask that attaches to her ventilator because she doesn't want to fuel taboos associated with the reliance on devices and machines. Her latest creative collaboration—Access is Love—asks us to rethink "accessibility" as something more than a legal or logistical burden. According to Alice, we should instead embrace accessibility as a shared value at the very heart of building a more just and caring society.

Creating something is the best antidote to feeling powerless in the face of oppression.

ALICE WONG
ACTIVIST

Dawn Shaughnessy

born 1975

SCI-FI BUFF • ULTRAMODERN SCIENCE INNOVATOR •
PERIODIC TABLE EXPANDER

Early on, Dawn Shaughnessy felt an affinity toward science. Her dad was an engineer. Her favorite toys were an electronics kit and a chemistry set. But it was the imaginative, no-limits mindset inspired by her love of science fiction that ultimately steered her into a career of barrier-breaking discoveries. The young Star Wars devotee took inspiration from that galaxy far, far away to wonder about the forces at work within our own. She initially imagined a future in orthopedic medicine, but her first awestruck encounter with the gigantic particle accelerators and laser beams of nuclear chemistry convinced her it was a field where science and science fiction could meld. Not only could she study atoms, she could create them using the world's most avant-garde tech. Dawn dove in and became a modern-day alchemist with a passion for synthesizing never-before-seen superheavy elements. As head of the experimental nuclear and radiochemistry group at Lawrence Livermore National Laboratory, she's rewritten the "Bible of Chemistry" by adding six elements—numbers 113–118—to the periodic table. One of them—#116—is even fondly named "Livermorium" after her home lab.

The heaviest known elements are not, so far as we know, found in nature. Instead, Dawn worked with international collaborators to manufacture them by smashing the atoms of two existing elements together. Forged in extreme conditions generated by some seriously enormous and expensive hardware, these atoms only last for the blink of an eye before busting apart. They may not have obvious practical applications now, but they do have profound theoretical implications. Dawn's ever-expanding list of new elements is her way to creatively test the limits of matter. She wants to understand why we have the atoms that we do and how they're held together. Today, you may well see the American Chemistry Society fellow sporting her custom-made Jedi robes as she continues to write her own epic STEM saga to see if there's a point where the periodic table ends. Her light saber may only be a prop, but there's no question that Dawn's at the cutting edge.

"

You have to suspend
in your mind what
is possible.

"

DAWN SHAUGHNESSY
NUCLEAR CHEMIST

DARINGLY

"If you risk nothing,
then you risk everything."

GEENA DAVIS
ACTOR

Annie Smith Peck

1850–1935

LATIN PROFESSOR • FIRSTS-CHASING CLIMBER •
UNOFFICIAL AMBASSADOR FOR SOUTH AMERICA

In 1911, at age 61, Annie Smith Peck led the first ascent of the Nevado Coropuna peak in Peru, planting a "Votes for Women" flag on the 21,079-foot-high summit. The intrepid suffragist had long been a model of female independence, following her globe-trotting impulses according to her own timeline. She'd already been teaching for years when she enrolled among the first female grad students at classics programs in Michigan and Athens. Studying abroad in Europe gave her a taste for the freedom of travel. Seeing the majestic, snowcapped Matterhorn gave her a hankering to climb it. After years of prep, at 45, the "sedate teacher of dead languages" and popular parlor lecturer in Greek and Roman archaeology put herself on the map as an audacious adventurer. She may have been the third woman to climb the Matterhorn, but she was the first bold enough to do it in pants! Her own family was so shocked by the display, they sent the rebuke, "If you are determined to commit suicide, why not come home and do so in a quiet, lady-like manner." Photos of Annie sporting the standard (male) climbing costume created a sensation. They were widely reprinted and even fashioned into trading cards to distribute with everything from cigarettes to Singer sewing machines.

But Annie wasn't content to be *among* the first women to achieve something. She turned her attention to South America's Andes Mountains, filled with peaks never explored by any living soul. On her sixth perilous attempt, she led the first expedition to summit Huascarán, descending to receive a medal from the Peruvian government and find that the mountain's northern peak had been renamed in her honor. Supporting her many treks with lecture tours billed as the "Queen of the Climbers" and publishers' advances for books and exclusive articles, Annie kept hiking mountains until age 82. She remains a muse for many a pathfinder. Even Amelia Earhart acknowledged: "I am only following in the footsteps of one who pioneered when it was brave just to put on the bloomers necessary for mountain-climbing."

❝

Climbing is unadulterated hard labor. The only real pleasure is the satisfaction of going where no man has been before and where few can follow.

❞

ANNIE SMITH PECK
MOUNTAINEER

Estée Lauder

1906–2004

BEAUTICIAN TURNED BUSINESS EXEC • PHILANTHROPIST • MARKETING GENIUS

Estée Lauder started her namesake company with four skin care products cooked up in the kitchen of a former New York restaurant. She retired as the world's wealthiest self-made woman, counting the likes of Grace Kelly, Nancy Reagan, and Frank Sinatra among her inner circle. It took a lot more than a pretty, perfectly moisturized face to get there. Estée got her start in the beauty industry when just a teen. Growing up over her father's hardware store in Queens, she learned the secrets of skin care from her Hungarian uncle—a chemist who would formulate creams in the cramped stable behind their house. A born saleswoman, Estée went around her neighborhood, offering free samples and doing demos for women while they were sitting under salon hair dryers, waiting for the subway, or lounging in hotel lobbies. After marrying her husband Joseph (for the second time), they decided to team up to take her vision to the next level. When Estée Lauder Cosmetics was officially founded in 1946, she and Joe comprised the entire company. Estée would sell during the day and handle the production at night. When she managed to coax Saks Fifth Ave into stocking her wares, they sold out in two days, opening the door to upscale department stores everywhere.

Always a hands-on leader who demanded excellence in both product and presentation, Estée would attend every store opening to personally oversee training and earned a reputation as a one-woman research department. Her outside-the-box brainchildren—like the luxurious yet affordable Youth Dew bath oil that doubled as perfume—and strokes of marketing genius—such as inventing the gift-with-purchase incentive—kept the company growing into a global leader. The Presidential Medal of Freedom honoree's beauty empire now spans 150 countries with 48,000 employees and $2 billion in annual revenue. Still a family affair, her heirs carry on their founder's daring vision and unflagging drive.

> **"**
>
> Serenity is pleasant, but it lacks the ecstasy of achievement. I've insisted on the long stretch rather than the gentle reach.
>
> **"**

ESTÉE LAUDER
COSMETICS MOGUL

Eugenie Clark

1922–2015

DEEP-SEA ADVENTURER • *NATIONAL GEOGRAPHIC* FELLOW
& COVER GIRL • THE "SHARK LADY"

Eugenie Clark forever made waves in her field by daring to study fish in their natural habitat—underwater. Her 72 submersible dives and more than 200 research trips to remote marine destinations from Borneo to Mexico were a far cry from her urban upbringing in New York City. Eugenie credited her ocean-centered Japanese heritage and weekends spent haunting the Battery Park Aquarium with sparking her urge to swim with sharks. She embarked on her first solo expedition as a Fulbright Scholar. Keen to tap into local knowledge, Eugenie took Red Sea spearfishers for her guides. Her 1953 memoir, recounting her feats and finds, became an international best seller and was so personally admired by the Vanderbilts that they offered to set the young ichthyologist up with her own Florida lab. Eugenie founded what would become the Mote Marine Laboratory in 1955. As director and later trustee, she took the institution from a single 12-by-20-foot room to a world-class research facility famous for ocean conservation and public outreach. Today it's home to 200 specialists, an aquarium, and the US's only official Center for Shark Research.

Eugenie's wide-ranging scientific adventures transformed our understanding of marine animals and their behavior. She discovered several species of fish and has several named after her—including a 2018 find, the adorably big-eyed *Squalus clarkae* or "Genie's dogfish." With a soft spot for sharks, she made breakthrough discoveries about how they slept, gave birth to live young, had impressive senses of memory, and were imminently trainable. Eugenie also doubled as a PR person for the genus. She filmed myth-busting documentaries, invited the author of *Jaws* on a dive, and even took a ride aback a 50-foot whale shark to refute their bad reps as mindless mankillers. She knew that protecting the ocean necessitated introducing people to its hidden wonders. With hundreds of popular articles, lectures, and demonstrations, plus more than 30 years of university teaching, Eugenie took many a future scientist under her flipper and left a throng of shark aficionados in her wake.

" I don't like repetitions... there is still so much to learn and experience! "

EUGENIE CLARK
DIVER & MARINE BIOLOGIST

Denise McCluggage

1927–2015

PRETEEN CAR ENTHUSIAST • PIONEERING SPORTS JOURNALIST • "THE FASTEST WOMAN IN AMERICA"

Denise McCluggage steered the way to a new style of sports journalism, covering the extreme sports beat by becoming one of its most daredevil participants. Like many female reporters in the 1950s, she regularly dealt with editors who were intent on keeping her confined to "women's features." With relentless determination, Denise talked and pitched (on the staff softball team), expertly skied, and thrillingly wrote her way into juicier assignments. Over the course of her pedal-to-the-metal career, she would take a turn at midget racing, parry as a champion fencer, and parachute from airplanes. But it was the up-and-coming sport of auto racing that stole her heart and made her name.

Denise had been a sports car enthusiast since the age of six. As an adult she lived as simply as possible—eating pasta every night in her studio apartment—so that she could afford to get behind the wheel of the world's flashiest rides. When Denise landed a Sunday racing feature with her dream paper, the *New York Herald Tribune*, it was often easier for women to enter the races themselves than the tracks' press boxes. Competing around the world in her signature white-and-red polka-dot crash helmet, she earned the nickname "Lady Leadfoot" as her syndicated column "Drive, She Said" spread to 90 newspapers. She motored an electric blue Ferrari Berlinetta to her most monumental victory, topping her class in the 1956 Sebring 12-hour Grand Prix of Endurance. As an exhilarating advocate, she helped get more women in gear with books like *Are You a "Woman Driver"?* As a respected insider, she became the first woman to cover the Indy 500 as well as a onetime owner and longtime writer for the magazine that would become *AutoWeek*. She remains the only journalist inducted into the Automotive Hall of Fame. For Denise, sports were not merely an adrenaline rush but a path to mindfulness. Her writings expressed the profound beauty of "those clear neon-lined moments of being truly tuned in." Her ultimate revelation? "The slower your breathe, the faster you go."

Change is the only constant. Hanging on is the only sin.

DENISE MCCLUGGAGE
RACE CAR DRIVER

Kathryn Bigelow

born 1951

SCREENWRITER, DIRECTOR & PRODUCER • INDIE AUTEUR •
1ST OSCAR-WINNING WOMAN DIRECTOR

Kathryn Bigelow's father was a small-town paint factory manager who mourned his unfulfilled dream of becoming a cartoonist. His stifled aspirations drew out his daughter's life ambition to be an artist. Kathryn excelled in art school and won a fellowship at the Whitney Museum of American Art in 1972. She moved to New York City, where she was mentored by Susan Sontag and bumped elbows with Andy Warhol. But soon the promising painter became frustrated with the limited appeal and reach of her canvases in comparison to the silver screen. Without any formal technical training, she made an intuitive leap into filmmaking.

Since then Kathryn has made an art of unsettling audiences and getting their adrenaline going. She's become one of the film industry's first major female directors while consciously maintaining the independent outsider status that has granted her immense creative control. From her first feature-length film—starring a then-unknown William Defoe as an outlaw biker—she pushed the boundaries of traditionally feminine subject matter and inventively bent genres. Her oeuvre includes everything from sci-fi noir to vampire westerns to period-piece thrillers. Her acclaimed 2008 film about a US Army bomb disposal squad in Iraq captured six Oscars, including Best Picture—quite a coup given that *The Hurt Locker*'s main rival had a $237 million budget to her $11 million. It also made her the first—and as of yet, only—woman to win the Academy Award for Best Director . . . a major feat in a profession with so vast a gender gap women account for less than 5% of directors on top-grossing films. Recently, Kathryn has translated her talents to high-impact documentaries, partnering with nonprofits to produce shorts on the illegal ivory trade, as well as the "I am not a Weapon" campaign featuring first-person testimonies from Nigerian girls who were kidnapped by Boko Haram terrorists. These projects harken back to why the young painter dared to switch mediums: her conviction that film remains one of our most powerful social tools for provoking reactions and prompting much-needed dialogue.

66

I don't want to be made pacified or made comfortable. I like stuff that gets your adrenaline going.

99

KATHRYN BIGELOW
FILMMAKER

FAITHFULLY

"Letting there be room for not knowing
is the most important thing of all."

PEMA CHÖDRÖN
BUDDHIST NUN

Elizabeth Ann Seton

1774–1821

NUN • CONVENT FOUNDER WHO FAITHFULLY SERVED THE POOR • 1ST AMERICAN TO BE CANONIZED

Elizabeth Ann Seton was born into a wealthy New York family on the eve of American independence. She married a prosperous import merchant at 19 and had five children. Their life seemed blessed until both her husband's health and business began to fail. The family traveled to Italy to help him recuperate, but soon after he died of tuberculosis. The devoutly Episcopalian Elizabeth was introduced to Catholicism while abroad. Taken with the Virgin Mary, she formally converted upon her return to the US. Prejudice against her newly found faith made it difficult to run the boys' boardinghouse she was depending upon for her family's livelihood. After struggling to get by, she was invited by priests to open a school for girls in Baltimore, the first of its kind for American Catholics. The project attracted devotees from around the country, who became the first initiates of the Sisters of Charity convent, founded by Elizabeth in 1809. Serving as mother superior of the order for 12 years, she instituted vows of poverty, chastity, obedience, and service to the poor. Besides running St. Joseph's Academy and Free School and ministering to the needy in their community, the sisters began expanding their mission to staff orphanages in New York and Philadelphia.

Elizabeth did not have a long life, but she left a lofty legacy. In 1975, enough people had attested to miracles—enacted by praying to Elizabeth to intercede on their behalf—that Pope Paul IV officially made her a saint, the very first born on American soil. As a devotee who found her calling across the ocean as a mourning wife, she's considered the holy protector of widows and seafarers. And as the originator of Catholic education in the US, she's also the patron saint of Catholic schools. Now entombed in a Maryland basilica, Elizabeth's national shrine remains a site of pilgrimage for many Roman Catholics. Readers of all beliefs continue to mine her collected journals, correspondence, and reflections as rich sources of spiritual wisdom and guidance that urge us to live humbly and serve others.

66

Live simply so that others may simply live.

99

ELIZABETH ANN SETON
SAINT

Thubten Chodron

born 1950

TEACHER TURNED ABBESS • MONASTERY FOUNDER •
LEADING LIGHT IN DHARMA OUTREACH

Thubten Chodron grew up as a "nice Jewish girl" in Chicago and LA. The urban elementary school teacher was searching for meaning and fulfillment when a flyer posted at a local bookstore caught her eye. She ended up attending the meditation course taught by two Tibetan lamas and had a spiritual "aha." Buddhism, with its emphasis on cultivating wisdom and compassion, immediately made sense to her ethically and intellectually. But it was the practice of the philosophy that gradually transformed Thubten's curiosity into wholehearted belief. In fact, the more she put the teachings into practice, the more centered she felt. Soon she was on the path to becoming a very different sort of teacher, living in monasteries in Nepal, India, and Taiwan to continue her studies and begin the hard work of making her behavior match her newly found values. Mentored by great Tibetan masters, including the Dalai Lama himself, Thubten officially became a nun in the Tibetan tradition in 1977 and received her full ordination as a *bhikshuni* (female monastic leader) in 1986. Still, she spent some years feeling adrift until she found her purpose: translating Buddhist traditions to speak to modern Western audiences.

There were plenty of meditation centers in the US, but she wanted to build a full-fledged monastery. When, in 2003, Thubten signed the mortgage on a 360-acre property in a rural corner of eastern Washington, she and her two cats were the sole residents. She had no idea how she was going to pay it off. Patience brought results. Thubten's Sravasti Abbey is not only the first US Tibetan Buddhist training monastery, it's also one of the few worldwide where women can be ordained. With a commitment to outreach, Thubten has developed programs for supporting prisoners and at-risk youth while writing or editing more than 40 popular books, including a series coauthored with the Dalai Lama. As more and more people turn to Thubten's community for insight and guidance, they're furthering her mission of creating peace in a chaotic world and an "energy field for the common good."

"

Abandon impatience and instead be content creating the causes for goodness; the results will come when they're ready.

"

THUBTEN CHODRON
BUDDHIST NUN

Joy Harjo

born 1951

INDIGENOUS RIGHTS ADVOCATE • MUSICIAN • 1ST NATIVE AMERICAN US POET LAUREATE

For Joy Harjo, becoming a poet was not only her calling, it was her salvation. Kicked out of her family home in Tulsa, Oklahoma, at age 16 by an abusive stepfather, by her early 20s she had already dealt with teen motherhood, drug addiction, poverty, and a failed marriage. She was stuck in a series of dead-end jobs when the "spirit of poetry" found her. "I needed to find my voice," she believes, "in order to live." Even at the lowest moments of her journey, Joy felt protected by her Muscogee Creek ancestors, but poetry became a path toward healing and overcoming the painful narratives imposed on her and her people. Adopting the last name of her painter grandmother, which means "crazy brave," Joy poured her newfound life force into the contemporary native art movement. In 2019, she became the first Native American to be appointed US poet laureate. The high-profile role has given Joy the chance to make visible the nation's indigenous roots, as well as reveal how our seemingly singular and disparate stories are deeply interconnected.

Over the course of her career as an acclaimed author, artist, and university educator, Joy's divine muse has expressed itself not only in books of poetry, memoir, and children's literature, but also through song. Music was Joy's first love. Her mother was a singer whose "heartbreak ballads" left a deep impression. The young artist began to see music as "a language that lives in the spiritual realms" and understand our sacred and everyday duty as carriers of those "voices, songs, and stories to grow and release into the world." She has written tracks for and toured with two all-native rock bands (Poetic Justice and Arrow Dynamics), releasing five albums and nabbing a NAMMY (Native American Music Award) for Best Female Artist in 2009. These days, her poetry readings are laced with alto sax solos . . . a nod to the birthplace of jazz being at the heart of her tribe's ancestral territories.

Every soul has a distinct song.

"

JOY HARJO
POET

Oprah Winfrey

born 1954

1ST WOMAN TO OWN HER OWN TALK SHOW • 1ST BLACK FEMALE
BILLIONAIRE • SUPER-SOUL GURU

Oprah Winfrey is one of the few people on a first-name basis with the world. We know her as a beloved talk show host (the highest rated of all time), an Oscar-nominated actor and producer who brings African American history to life, a tastemaker whose picks steer popular demand, the mogul of a media empire who founded her own network, and a philanthropist who's donated hundreds of millions to everything from education for underprivileged girls to the Smithsonian's newest addition—the National Museum of African American History and Culture. Genuine and empathetic, yet outspoken when the occasion demands it, she's become something of a modern-day prophet for calling "time's up" on those barriers that keep people from living their best lives. She's also a 21st-century spiritual leader with a deeply personal take on religion.

Raised by her Mississippi grandmother as a toddler, Oprah had a Southern Baptist upbringing. As an 8-year-old, she took her baptism so seriously that her third-grade classmates dubbed her "the preacher girl." She's since acknowledged that turning to God helped her through the many trials of her troubled childhood, from poverty to abuse that led to an early pregnancy before she even knew what being pregnant meant. Today, Oprah still prays every night in the way her grandma taught her. To this "ritual of reverence" she's added her own soul-nourishing regime. Besides striving to be present in the moment, she takes time each morning to be still and center herself before leaping into her inevitably packed itinerary. A firm believer in the power of gratitude, she keeps a daily log of things she's grateful for and gives thanks to God for even the most banal blessings throughout the day. Most importantly, Oprah expresses her faith through helping others become more of who they were created to be. Launching popular programs like *SuperSoul Sunday*, producing documentary series like *Belief*, and keynoting at the likes of Stanford's Divinity School are a few of the ways that this open-minded evangelist is enabling connections to the spirit.

"I'm not telling you what to believe, or who to believe, or what to call it, but there is no full life, no fulfilled, meaningful, sustainably joyful life without a connection to the spirit."

OPRAH WINFREY
MEDIA MOGUL

Terry Tempest Williams

born 1955

NATURAL HISTORY MUSEUM CURATOR • FAITH-FILLED AUTHOR •
"STORYTELLER, DISRUPTOR, ENGAGED CITIZEN"

Raised in Utah's Salt Lake Valley, Terry Tempest Williams learned to cherish its dark sky full of stars and "the curvature of the Earth in an erosional landscape." An acclaimed environmental writer steeped in the American West, she's descended from Mormon pioneers and grew up with their faith traditions. While it has been years since she belonged to any church, she still honors her religious background for giving her a deep appreciation of community, family, and place. Those are the love-centered values she wants to take seed through her work.

A naturalist and educator first, Terry didn't set out to have a career in writing. She learned the art of storytelling as a young science teacher whose students flourished when she could translate biology and geology lessons into awe-inspiring narratives. Her first published work, the National Science Foundation Book Award winner *The Secret Language of Snow,* was for children. Turning to the fraught tale of her own native landscape, Terry emerged as a giant of American nature writing with the 1991 memoir *Refuge.* Now a widely published master of creative nonfiction with a conscience, she's lent her lyrical voice to meditations on everything from erosion to democracy, earned multiple accolades—from a Guggenheim fellowship to the Sierra Club's John Muir Award—and served as a professor or writer-in-residence everywhere from the University of Utah to Harvard's Divinity School. To mark the centennial of the National Park Service, she appeared in a Ken Burns documentary series and penned a "personal topography" of US national parks, including her time teaching in the Grand Tetons. Terry has also pledged to put her boots on the ground as an activist, protesting aboveground nuclear testing and starting her own energy company so she could buy up leases to prevent fossil fuel drilling on public lands. Today the eco-author is helping the world see climate change as a spiritual issue. Addressing it means adopting an ethical stance that respects the worth of all living things while acting on a selfless devotion to the well-being of future generations.

"

The eyes of our future
are looking back at us,
and they are praying
for us to see beyond our
own time.

"

TERRY TEMPEST WILLIAMS
CONSERVATIONIST

FIERCELY

"I am not lucky. You know what I am?
I am smart, I am talented, I take advantage
of the opportunities that come my way
and I work really, really hard.
Don't call me lucky. Call me a badass."

SHONDA RHIMES
WRITER-PRODUCER

Louisa May Alcott

1832–1888

The often disgruntled daughter of a pretty, high-society mother and a penniless, scholarly father, Louisa May Alcott grew up in a community of leading US thinkers, learning from the likes of Henry David Thoreau, Margaret Fuller, and Ralph Waldo Emerson. Her philosopher father had radical ideas about education, sinking the family's small income into founding ill-fated utopian communes and establishing schools that were too far-out to keep their doors open for long. Before the aspiring author became one of the country's best-loved names in children's literature, Louisa moonlighted as an actress, laundress, lady's companion, seamstress, and governess to make ends meet. During the Civil War, the staunch abolitionist served unflinchingly as a Union nurse; she signed on as a suffragist after. But through all her hard work at various grinding labors and good causes, Louisa kept up her main passion—writing.

Sitting at the shelf desk her dad built for her in their Concord, Massachusetts, home, Louisa would scribble late into the night. She made a small income turning out fanciful and pulpy short stories. It wasn't until she published *Little Women*—a fictionalized account of her own New England childhood—that she became a household name. The novel's first volume came out in 1868, complete with illustrations by Louisa's artist sister May. An immediate hit, 2,000 copies flew off the shelves. The following year, when a second volume was slated to be published seeing the girls into adulthood, Louisa received heaps of fan mail telling her how the story should end. Spoiler alert—she resolutely refused to indulge the popular demand to have her Louisa-like protagonist get hitched to Laurie, the book's most obvious heartthrob. Today, the chronicles of the imaginative tomboy Jo and her three beloved sisters continue to delight audiences in multiple adaptations—including a 2019 reboot by acclaimed filmmaker Greta Gerwig and an all-star cast of feminists, from Saoirse Ronan to Emma Watson to Meryl Streep.

I like good strong words that mean something.

LOUISA MAY ALCOTT
AUTHOR

Mary Harris Jones

1837–1930

TEACHER & DRESSMAKER • UNION ORGANIZER •
"THE MOST DANGEROUS WOMAN IN AMERICA"

Mary Jones's early life was defined by personal encounters with epic historic tragedies: the Potato Famine that drove her family from Ireland to Canada; the 1867 yellow fever epidemic that swept across Tennessee, claiming the lives of her husband and four children; the Great Fire of 1871 that burned down the young widow's house and thriving Chicago dress shop. Mary rose from the ashes by dedicating her life to others, becoming known as the mother to millions of working people. As the growing pains of industrialization intensified, it left masses of workers struggling with low pay, long hours, dangerous working conditions, and no benefits. Mary began organizing them to collectively improve their lot. Adopting the mantra, "pray for the dead, and fight like hell for the living," she emerged out of grief and obscurity to become one of the most feared and admired women of her day.

Cultivating the persona of "Mother Jones," perpetually clad in antique black dresses with lace collars, the 5-foot-tall firebrand used her granny status to get away with razor-sharp rhetoric and shame her "children" into action. She made her home wherever she was needed, supporting strikes and union organizing campaigns from Pittsburgh steelworkers to El Paso streetcar operators. She grew the membership of the United Mine Workers from 10,000 to 300,000, coordinating miners' wives into "mop and broom brigades." She wasn't afraid to get arrested, be banned from cities, or take on the country's most powerful moguls, from JP Morgan to John D. Rockefeller. In one of her best-publicized stratagems, she led a 1903 march of 100 child silk workers in Philadelphia all the way to President Theodore Roosevelt's summer home on Long Island. With poignant rallies at every stop along the way, Mary raised awareness about child labor and made it front-page news. Never keen on suffragism (because she didn't think voting could really affect change), the mother-to-all was still well ahead of her time in warmly inviting women, children, and minorities to join in the labor movement's efforts to forge more equal futures.

I'm not a humanitarian, I'm a hell-raiser.

MOTHER JONES
LABOR ORGANIZER

Virginia Apgar

1909–1974

ANESTHETIST & INVENTOR • MARCH OF DIMES RESEARCH DIRECTOR • GODMOTHER OF NEONATAL CARE

From the time she was a kid, the fast-talking, fast-thinking Virginia Apgar was known for her boundless energy. "Frankly, how does she do it?" asked her high school yearbook editor, before Virginia headed off to college, where she competed in seven sports, acted in theatricals, wrote for the newspaper, played violin in the orchestra, and earned top honors in her zoology major. She took that vim with her to med school, where she graduated fourth in her class, going on to do a residency in surgery. Though she greatly impressed her adviser at Presbyterian Hospital, he worried that she'd have trouble getting ahead as a female surgeon during the Great Depression. Taking his advice, Virginia made her mark in the emerging field of anesthesiology instead. In 1938, she returned to Presbyterian as its first female department head and the director of the division of anesthesia at Columbia's med school, where she'd eventually be appointed its first female full professor.

During her tenure in medicine, Virginia helped establish anesthesiology as a recognized specialty, overseen for the first time by physicians. Her most enduring contributions were to obstetrics and the care of infants. In the 1950s, she developed a method for quickly evaluating newborns' key vital signs. The Apgar Score was adopted as standard procedure around the world and still is decades later. Besides lowering infant mortality, Virginia's system helped to assess the effects of labor, delivery, and anesthetic practices on a baby's health. Having attended 17,000 deliveries over the course of her career, the doctor couldn't help growing increasingly concerned about birth defects. She decided to enroll in a master's of public health program and wound up joining the staff of the March of Dimes as an advocate and public educator on birth defect prevention and research. The vivacious Virginia was so skilled at the role, she more than doubled the organization's income. On duty wherever she went, the stalwart lifesaver was said to always carry a resuscitation kit so that no one would stop breathing on her watch.

66

Nobody, but nobody, is going to stop breathing on me!

99

VIRGINIA APGAR
PHYSICIAN

Fannie Lou Hamer

1917–1977

SHARECROPPER • VOTING RIGHTS CAMPAIGNER • NATIONAL WOMEN'S POLITICAL CAUCUS COFOUNDER

The youngest of 20 children, Fannie Lou Hamer started to work the fields with her family when she was six years old. By 12, she'd left school to pick cotton full-time, eventually becoming a plantation timekeeper. In 1961, Fannie went in for a minor surgery and woke up with a full hysterectomy undertaken without her knowledge or consent. This sterilizing practice was so common with African American women in her state, it was known as a "Mississippi appendectomy." The experience shocked Fannie into action. Signing on as a voting rights organizer, her initial attempt to register herself and 17 others was denied due to a bogus literacy test, and sparked immediate retaliation. Their driver was arrested on the way home for his bus being "too yellow," Fannie was fired, and her new residence shot at. Soon after successfully registering to vote in 1963, she was arrested for violating segregation laws and beaten so brutally it left lasting damage. Intimidation tactics made Fannie more fiercely determined to fight for civil rights and bring as many people as she could along under the banner of freedom.

She earned a reputation as a charismatic, no-holds-barred speaker. At the 1964 Democratic National Convention the party so feared the impact of her testimony, they arranged a last-minute televised press conference with their presidential candidate to prevent its being broadcast. The move gave Fannie's speech more publicity, and by the time the next convention rolled around, her demand for parity and integration of delegations had been met. Fed up with the slow pace of politics, Fannie began dreaming up ways to immediately improve the daily lives of her community. Besides coordinating relief work and organizing plaintiffs for precedent-setting desegregation lawsuits, she launched economic empowerment initiatives, like a "pig bank" to give away free stock and a 640-acre cooperative farm with an associated store, boutique, and sewing wing. Her life was cut short by chronic ill-health, but the late-breaking activist kept fighting until her last breath.

"I don't want to hear you say, 'Honey, I'm behind you.' Well, move, I don't want you back there. Because you could be 200 miles behind. I want you to say, 'I'm with you.' And we'll go up this freedom road together."

FANNIE LOU HAMER
CIVIL RIGHTS LEADER

Beyoncé Knowles

born 1981

SINGER-SONGWRITER • HIGHEST-PAID BLACK RECORDING ARTIST
OF ALL TIME • GIRL WHO RUNS THE WORLD

Beyoncé Knowles's parents detected a talent for singing and dancing in their shy daughter, but they didn't realize how deep her passion ran for performing until they saw how she lit up on stage. After seeing her win her first talent contest at age seven, Beyoncé's parents went all-in, supporting her extraordinary determination to make it to the big time. By 17, Beyoncé had cowritten her first hit song and formed the all-female singing group, managed by her father, that would become Destiny's Child. They landed a deal with Columbia Records in 1997, ruling the R&B scene and selling 40 million albums. But it wasn't until she went solo in 2003 that fans first saw the uninhibited, booty-shaking Beyoncé—a persona she'd later dub "Sasha Fierce"—step out onto the mainstage. Beyoncé's debut solo record *Dangerously in Love* hit the sweet spot with fans and critics, going platinum and winning five Grammys. She hasn't slowed down since, hustling her way to global superstardom. Besides headlining two Super Bowls, she's become the most-nominated woman in Grammy history. With her 2016 release *Lemonade,* she also became the only person ever to have their first six albums debut at #1.

Beyoncé has admitted that her evolution as an artist has also been a personal journey, from striving to please others to learning how to please herself. Along the way, she decided it was high time to be her own boss and launched her Parkwood Entertainment production company to make that happen. Now a bona fide mogul hailed as Queen Bey, the singer-songwriter has created her own fragrance and clothing lines, produced and starred in multiple movies including the recent live-action reboot of *The Lion King,* and signed emerging talent to her label. Her hard-earned advice to the fresh acts she's taking under her wing? Don't compromise your art for the sake of gaining an audience. As Beyoncé's music has become more experimental, her performances and priorities have shifted toward empowering communities and leveling the playing field.

> "Don't try to lessen yourself for the world; let the world catch up with you."

BEYONCÉ
POP ICON

FREELY

"Independence is happiness."

SUSAN B. ANTHONY
SUFFRAGIST

Hallie Morse Daggett

1878–1964

RUGGED OUTDOORS-GIRL • 1ST FEMALE US FOREST SERVICE HIRE • ARDENT NATURE PROTECTOR

In 1913, the US Forest Service decided to take a chance on one of the "most untiring and enthusiasti[c] applicants" they'd ever had for any position. That "wide-awake woman of 30 years . . . not afraid of any[-] thing that walks, creeps, or flies" was Hallie Daggett, daughter of a mine owner turned superintenden[t] of the San Francisco Mint. Hired as a "forest guard," she earned $840 per year and had two days off pe[r] month. Her first post at Eddy's Gulch Lookout Station—6,444 feet up and a solid three-hours' hard climb from anywhere—was a far cry from the affluent city life she'd left behind. Hallie didn't mind. She ha[d] been raised in the Salmon River watershed, learning to ride, hunt, fish, and trap as she, her sister, an[d] brother explored the rugged Siskiyou Mountains. Her tiny, solitary mountaintop cabin—with only marauc[d]-ing wildlife and her seven pet chipmunks for company—felt like a glorious escape from "the imprisonin[g] habitations of Civilization." During her first season, she reported some 40 fires. Hallie's early detectio[n] meant fewer than five acres in total burned. The Forest Service declared their experimental hiring of a lad[y] lookout to be a roaring success, anticipating the day when the majority of US lookouts would be women[.]

Hallie put in 14 more years of service, savoring each post as a scenic getaway while relishing th[e] chance to do her part in protecting and conserving the forests she loved. During her tenure, the trailblaz[-]ing outdoorswoman kindled plenty of public interest. Sensationalist stories about her living alone in th[e] wilderness, braving treacherous electrical storms, and taking out prowling coyotes appeared in print acros[s] the nation, from the *San Francisco Call* to the *Boston Globe*. She was even asked to be the subject of a[n] early motion picture. Hallie knew the slow pace of her patient, ever-vigilant work was out of step with th[e] nonstop demands of modern careers, but, to her, the view—stretching from Mount Shasta to the distan[t] sparkle of the Pacific—was never monotonous. "I like it; I love it!" she said, "And that's why I'm here."

"

Outdoors—all outdoors—was a grander dooryard than any estate in the land could boast, and oh! what a prospect of glorious freedom from four walls and a time-clock.

"

HALLIE DAGGETT
FIRE LOOKOUT

Ruth Faison Shaw

1889–1969

SELF-TAUGHT ARTS EDUCATOR • PROGRESSIVE SCHOOL FOUNDER • PATENT-HOLDING INVENTOR

Arts educator Ruth Faison Shaw created a sensation when she introduced finger painting to the United States in the 1930s. Though the general technique had been used before, Ruth was the first to develop it into a popular educational and therapeutic tool. An intuitive educator, she'd jumped into teaching in a rural Appalachian classroom without any official qualifications. After serving as a YMCA canteen worker in France during WWI, she remained abroad to open her own primary school for English-speaking students in Rome. It was during her decade running the Shaw School that Ruth first hatched the idea for finger painting. She had sent a boy with a cut finger to put some iodine on it. When he didn't return, she found him doodling on the bathroom wall with impressive smears of anti-septic. Instead of being upset, Ruth was inspired. She realized he'd shown her a fun and instinctual way for children to express themselves. She spent a few years devising the best method and perfecting her formula for a safe, nontoxic paint before heading back to the US as a gung ho finger-painting advocate. When her pupils put on the first exhibition of finger painting, it earned a rave review in the *New York Times* and scored Ruth a book deal to introduce the art to nationwide audiences. When the handicraft company that would become Crayola began manufacturing Shaw Finger Paints, they hired her to demo them around the country. In the 1940s, Ruth found new purposes for her signature art as a rehabilitation method. Working with WWII soldiers and mentally challenged patients, she explored its power to draw out hidden fears and incite emotional releases.

Today, finger painting may seem like an obvious invention, but it marked a major turning point in the field of education. Ruth's lessons encouraged freedom, creativity, and self-expression over discipline, accurate replication, or rote memorization. Never prompting people what to create, she invited everyone to boldly improvise, not just with their fingertips, but also with their knuckles, palms, fists, and even whole forearms.

Be very free with your motions and bold with your colors.

RUTH FAISON SHAW
MOTHER OF FINGER PAINTING

Amelia Earhart

1897–1937? (officially declared dead in 1939)

SERIAL RECORD-SETTER • PR MAGNET & PUBLIC RELATIONS VP • "THE FIRST LADY OF FLIGHT"

"I want to do it because I want to do it," wrote Amelia Earhart to husband George Putnam in the letter she left behind before taking off on what would be her last flight. Her whole life, she had freely followed that adventurous instinct of doing precisely what she wanted, whether it be riding "belly-whopper" style down a Kansas sledding hill as a kid or setting out to become the first woman (and second person) to fly solo across the Atlantic. It was an instinct that cost the aviation pioneer her life—when her custom-built Lockheed Electra was lost forever somewhere over the Pacific during her daring 1937 attempt to circumnavigate the world. But it also landed her an enduring place in the public's imagination.

Amelia may be a figurehead for unapologetically following the "inner desire of your heart," but that doesn't mean she didn't encounter plenty of turbulence along the way. A dysfunctional family life meant fending for herself and constant moves. When she fell bomber-hat-over-heels for flying at a 1920 Long Beach air show, she took on every odd job she could, from stenographer to photographer to truck driver, to fund lessons. She became the 16th woman to earn her pilot's license in 1923, but soon after had to sell her secondhand plane to abet family finances. She had done stints as a teacher, social worker, airplane sales rep, and local journalist in Boston when she finally got her big break in 1928—a last-minute invite to become the first woman to fly across the Atlantic . . . as a passenger. Her wholehearted "yes" saw her make history while soaring to the status of international celebrity and trendsetter. Amelia's highly publicized adventures established her as a brand (complete with her own practical-chic clothing and luggage lines) while garnering recognition for the causes she backed—like a women's pilot association named the Ninety-Nines and the ERA. A popular columnist, best-selling author, and founding airline exec, this ambassador of the air raised the professional prospects of her sex and the entire flying industry.

"

Who would refuse an invitation to such a shining adventure?

AMELIA EARHART
PILOT

Alice Coachman

1923–2014

TRACK-AND-FIELD LEGEND • 1ST BLACK WOMAN TO WIN OLYMPIC GOLD • GUTSY WAY-FINDER

Alice Coachman didn't like anyone to beat her. In elementary school, she quashed the boasts of boy challengers by besting them in race after race at recess. As a teen, she became the first African American woman to dominate the national track-and-field circuit. Each victory was a testament to her winning mindset: she was going to succeed in spite of the barriers and silence the doubters with her indisputable excellence. Growing up in segregated Georgia, it was tough to practice her passion. She was barred from using public sports facilities for training and often denied entry into events, but a boys' track coach finally took notice of her talent. After nabbing her first win on the Amateur Athletic Union (AAU) circuit—competing barefoot—when she was just 14, Alice landed full scholarships to the Tuskegee Institute and Albany State, pulling in a total of 25 national AAU championships. By 1946, she held the US title in four events: the 50- and 100-meter races, 400-meter relay, and high jump. WWII canceled the 1940 and 1944 Olympics, but 1948 brought Alice's moment to make history. She arrived at the London Games to find an enormous European fan base: 82,000 spectators showed up to watch the superstar narrowly secure a victory with an Olympic-record-setting jump. She came away as the first black woman to top the podium and the only American woman to take gold during that Games.

On the world's biggest sporting stage, Alice was personally presented with her medal by the king of England, George IV. When she returned to the States, she was mobbed by reporters, invited to the White House, and offered an endorsement deal with Coca-Cola (the first African American signed). Yet, her own hometown mayor refused to shake her hand during their segregated celebration of her remarkable achievements. Alice not only lived to see better times, she helped bring them about as a teacher, coach, and foundation founder who spurred on the next generation of gutsy barefoot kid athletes.

"I didn't worry about anything because I said, 'If I can do it, I'll do it.' And I had guts enough to do it."

ALICE COACHMAN
HIGH JUMPER

Halima Aden

born 1997

SOMALI REFUGEE • 1ST HIJAB-WEARING COVER GIRL •
UNICEF GOODWILL AMBASSADOR

In 2018, Halima Aden returned to the refugee camp in Kenya where she was born. There, she revealed her unlikely journey, from a girl fleeing civil war and dealing with malaria and hunger to an elite international model, racking up bookings around the globe. It was a story about hope but also about learning to be herself again. Conditions at Camp Kakuna were tough, yet kids of all backgrounds banded together to play and learn. When Halima's family was given the go-ahead to move to the US, the 7-year-old suddenly felt pressure to hide her differences and became wary of visually marking her Muslim faith. In 2016, she decided it was time to reclaim her identity and make a public statement about her choice to dress modestly as a part of her religious practice. She entered the Miss Minnesota USA beauty pageant, becoming the only contestant ever to take the stage in a hijab and sport a burkini for the swimsuit competition. She didn't come away with the tiara, but she did make national headlines.

Soon after, Halima was approached by a modeling agency. She had unprecedented provisos that stood a high likelihood of souring the deal: wearing the hijab at all times, never modeling clothing that revealed any skin, and always having an all-female support team. To her surprise, the agency execs agreed and enthusiastically signed her. Since then, Halima has posed her way to many historic firsts as the inaugural hijab-wearing model of high fashion. She has graced the cover of British *Vogue*, anchored a dazzling burkini spread in the *Sports Illustrated Swimsuit Edition,* and ruled the runways at Milan and New York Fashion Weeks for the likes of Max Mara, Zendaya, and Tommy Hilfiger. An icon of the diversifying face of fashion, Halima has become a catwalk staple. Yet, for her, the runway is above all a humanitarian platform. The proud black, Muslim Somali American from Kenya is using it to spread a message of cultural acceptance, celebrate our era of female empowerment, and better the lives of fellow refugees.

"What a great time to be yourself."

HALIMA ADEN
MODEL

GRACEFULLY

"I dwell in Possibility."

EMILY DICKINSON
POET

Annie Turnbo Malone

1869–1957

INVENTOR • MOTHER OF THE BLACK BEAUTY INDUSTRY • FAITH-FILLED PHILANTHROPIST

Orphaned young and incapacitated by sickness for much of her childhood, Annie Turnbo Malone was nevertheless strong-minded and stouthearted. She was fascinated by chemistry and loved doing up her sisters' hair. When a rage hit for straightening black hair in the 1890s—at the time, a gesture of progress toward freedom and equality—Annie seized the chance to translate the popular style into an industry. Working with her herbalist aunt, she developed a chemical hair straightener that—unlike homemade methods, which involved everything from goose fat to potatoes mixed with lye—did not damage scalps or hair follicles. The invention of her business model was more ingenious still. She launched her company Poro in St. Louis, Missouri, where there was an economic surge in anticipation of the 1904 World's Fair. Excluded from the normal retail channels, she devised a direct distribution system run by an army of sales agents—a strategy still used by cosmetics giants today. Annie's early team included future rival Madam CJ Walker; legendary rocker Chuck Berry joined up later. In 1918, she opened the US's first black cosmetology school. Besides training over 75,000 entrepreneurs, Poro College was a vital social venue for St. Louis's sizable black community.

In her heyday, Annie was one of the nation's richest African Americans. Yet, her cosmetics empire was never about personal wealth. Besides helping thousands of women gain confidence and financial independence, she lived simply and gave generously, granting endowments and scholarships to black universities while spearheading philanthropic efforts, like building a black YWCA and orphanage. (The latter is now a children and family service center, named after her.) After she stepped back from managing the business, it was nearly sunk by costly lawsuits and tax bills. But speaking at her last commencement ceremony in 1956, Annie remained an altruistic voice of optimism. She advised grads that investing in their communities and ensuring each member their dignity is just a "small down payment" on abundant personal and social returns.

"
People will encourage
and patronize you if you
have faith in them.

ANNIE TURNBO MALONE
ENTREPRENEUR

Julia Morgan

1872–1957

CIVIL ENGINEER • CASTLE DESIGNER • POSTHUMOUS AMERICAN INSTITUTE OF ARCHITECTS GOLD MEDALIST

Big-name architects of the early 20th century lived life with a flourish, commanding attention by being flamboyant self-promoters. The diminutive and bespectacled Julia Morgan, the first woman to earn an architect's license in California, took the opposite tack. She chose to let her life's work speak—and literally stand—for itself. Her design and engineering chops were heralded when her first major work, the Spanish Mission-style bell tower at Mills College, withstood an earthquake's fury, in part due to her innovative use of reinforced concrete. So when the Great San Francisco Earthquake of 1906 left Julia's hometown scorched and in rubble, the owners of the Fairmont Hotel came calling. The luxe hotel, just days from its grand opening, had sustained massive damage. When the painstaking restoration was completed a year later, a reporter assumed Julia's work was reflected in the tasteful interior decor. She deftly corrected him: her contribution was structural.

Julia was well-prepped for her career. The only woman to earn a civil engineering degree from UC Berkeley in 1894, she went on to apply to the École des Beaux-Arts in Paris, the world's most prestigious architecture school. Though she failed the entrance exam twice, the confident Julia kept going back to the drawing board until she got in, graduated, and secured an apprenticeship with a Parisian atelier. Philanthropist Phoebe Apperson Hearst offered to help underwrite Julia's education. Though her assistance was graciously declined, Phoebe's faith in Julia's abilities proved a lifelong gift. When she hired Julia to design one of the first YWCA buildings, it led to 29 more "Y" commissions. Julia's portfolio of 700+ projects was largely built through the support of an emerging network of female philanthropists, activists, and working women. One of her best referrals was Phoebe's son, newspaper tycoon William Randolph Hearst, who tapped Julia as architect—and construction foreperson—on what would become her 28-years-in-the-making masterpiece: the Hearst Castle at San Simeon. Today many "Julia Morgans" are still standing, proof positive that sturdy genius will outlast many a flashy trend.

Your faith in me is enough of a gift.

"

JULIA MORGAN
MASTER ARCHITECT

Helen "Penny" Chenery

1922–2017

WWII RED CROSS VOLUNTEER • BUSINESS-SCHOOL DROPOUT TURNED BUSINESS EXEC • "GRANDE DAME OF RACING"

Penny Chenery came to own the horse that would define her career in a coin toss with a fellow breeder. She lost. He got his first pick of their stock, and she got Secretariat, the foal that would mature into one of the finest Thoroughbreds in racing history. When Secretariat wowed the nation with his legendary 1973 Triple Crown title, she realized what a moment of grace that coin toss had been, but it also took uncommon grit to get to those grandstands. Penny's father was a public utilities tycoon and horse lover. She'd grown up riding but never had more than a nominal role in his breeding and racing operation. He'd bought Meadow Stables—a 2,600-acre spread in Virginia—in 1936. Thirty years later, the Denver stay-at-home mom realized her father and his stables were in trouble. His wife had died, and the onset of Alzheimer's meant he needed full-time care. Penny's siblings wanted to sell the farm and its 130 horses, but she was keen to carry on her dad's legacy. They reluctantly agreed to let her take the reins. In 1972, after many financial struggles, she came up with a big winner. Riva Ridge took both the Kentucky Derby and the Belmont Stakes. The Meadow was not only saved, it soon became the most famous racing outfit in the country.

The very next year, Penny and her super-horse Secretariat sprinted into nationwide acclaim. No horse had won the Triple Crown since 1948. Her strapping chestnut colt not only swept the classic races, his 31-length victory at the Belmont Stakes still ranks among the greatest feats in any sport. As a tough and charming spokeswoman, Penny emerged as the female figurehead and ambassador of a male-dominated arena. For the rest of her life, she continued to advocate for horse welfare and invite all walks of people into the racing tribe. In 2010, Penny reentered the spotlight as the subject of a winning Disney drama that shared her story of grit and grace with the world.

"

It's such a simple thing, sharing. Don't be a small tribe.

"

PENNY CHENERY
RACEHORSE OWNER & BREEDER

Jacqueline Kennedy Onassis

1929–1994

SOCIETY GIRL • FASHION & CULTURE ICON • ENVOY FOR ARTS, LITERATURE & HISTORIC PRESERVATION

In 1961, at just 31, Jackie Kennedy became a US first lady. Less than three years later, she'd become the world's most famous widow when President John F. Kennedy was shot and killed as she rode with him in an open car. Widely admired before her husband's assassination, the public veneration reached new heights with her display of courage and dignity during the state funeral she'd helped arrange. Though her time as first lady was tragically brief, she left an enduring legacy. With her trendsetting style and quietly engaging manner, Jackie was a not-so-secret weapon on the campaign trail and a multilingual diplomatic asset afterward. Always an art lover and history buff, Jackie made it her mission to transform the White House's public rooms into a celebration of US history through restoration and thoughtful curation. When she invited citizens to take a televised tour of the newly renovated residence, 80 million Americans tuned in. The landmark broadcast nabbed the skillful host an honorary Emmy.

Jackie may have been one of the most admired and photographed women in the world—popularizing everything from the pillbox hat to oversize sunglasses—but she was also one of the more reserved and elusive. Though she frequently found herself in the eye of a media storm, she rarely gave interviews. In 1975, the millionaire was hired at $200 a week to be a consulting editor. It was her first paying job since her two-year stint as the *Washington Times-Herald*'s "Inquiring Camera Girl" fresh out of college. Jackie calmly waded through the press circus without comment, went up to her small office, and proceeded to spend the last 19 years of her life in publishing. She shepherded nearly 100 books to market but pointedly refused to capitalize on her personal story. Never so much as keeping a journal, Jackie balanced out the demands of gracious global celebrity by living life in the present and keeping as much as she could of it as her own.

> "
> I want to live my life,
> not record it.
> "

JACKIE KENNEDY
FIRST LADY

Aesha Ash

born 1977

TRAILBLAZING CLASSIC DANCER • PRO BONO BALLET TEACHER • INSPIRER OF SWAN DREAMS

Aesha Ash was an inner-city kid who happened upon an unexpected calling. Raised in Rochester, New York, she started dancing jazz and tap at age five and was soon dominating the competition circuit. But the more trophies she earned, the less interested she got. When she made the switch to ballet, it was like discovering another side of herself—subtle, poised, and serene. Being a ballerina felt right, even if she didn't fit the alabaster mold of most classical dancers. By the time she turned 14, the School of American Ballet had come knocking with a scholarship. Four years later, she'd been dubbed a student of outstanding promise and pirouetted her way to a spot on the full-time corps of the New York City Ballet. After seven years as the troupe's only black ballerina, Aesha signed on as a soloist for celebrated companies in Switzerland and San Francisco before retiring at 29 to raise a family.

In 2011, the mother of two decided to lace up her toe shoes again. Only this time, she'd perform not on vaunted international stages but on the roughest streets of her hometown. Aesha launched the Swan Dreams Project, a self-designed and self-funded program of ballet outreach to encourage disadvantaged kids to freely imagine and aspire. Besides putting on free camps and classes in dance, nutrition, etiquette, and arts education, she started a photo campaign to break down the barriers between her two worlds. Capturing powerful, multidimensional representations of women of color, the images document impromptu performances in full ballet regalia at barbershops, bus stops, and schools. A picture of two little girls joyfully mimicking her motions on the sidewalk went viral—one of the many times Aesha's felt like she made an impact just by showing up. Today, the muse in a tutu is expanding her outreach to other cities to make an elegant point: "Beauty and grace are not defined by status or race. They are boundless."

> **You never know the impact you can have just by being a presence.**

AESHA ASH
BALLERINA

HONORABLY

"We have fought for America with all her imperfections, not so much for what she is, but for what we know she can be."

MARY MCLEOD BETHUNE
UNIVERSITY FOUNDER

Abigail Adams

1744–1818

FARM MANAGER • THE US'S 1ST SECOND LADY & 2ND FIRST LADY • POLITICAL INFLUENCER

Abigail Adams was the wife of the second US president and mother of its sixth. She was also the first first lady to take on hostess duties at the freshly constructed White House in the nation's new capital. But Abigail played more than a ceremonial role in the life of the young nation. In fact, her reputation as a political influencer was so strong that her husband's bid for reelection was lost in part for fear that the country was really being run by "Mrs. President." Largely self-educated, she grew up a prodigious reader, bonding with her future husband John—then a Harvard grad about to launch a legal career—over books. When the couple moved to his small family estate south of Boston, she raised their children and managed their farm and business investments while he traveled as a lawyer, circuit judge, revolutionary, diplomat, and politician. The couple's voluminous correspondence, in which they refer to one another as "My Dearest Friend," is filled with wit, wisdom, and tenderness that attest to their genuine union of heart and mind. It's also one of the most insightful and fascinating records we have of the American Revolution and early days of the republic. In her most famous message, Abigail demanded that John and his fellow lawmakers "Remember the Ladies" as he attended the First Continental Congress in 1776.

Abigail's letters were published by her grandson in 1848, and new editions of them are still being released today. Her historic pen pals include a who's who of US founders from Thomas Jefferson to Dolley Madison. Though she didn't live to see her son John Quincy in the White House, her lengthy missives to him reveal how seriously she took her duty of fostering his honorable development as a future leader. In one highly instructive 1778 letter, she cautioned him to always put virtue before talent and "stamp upon [his] mind this certain Truth, that the welfare and prosperity of all countries, communities and I may add individuals depend upon their Morals."

"Great Learning and superior abilities, should you ever possess them, will be of little value and small Estimation, unless Virtue, Honour, Truth and integrity are added to them."

ABIGAIL ADAMS
FIRST LADY

Mary Edwards Walker

1832–1919

SUFFRAGIST & DRESS REFORMER • PRISONER OF WAR • 1ST FEMALE US MEDAL OF HONOR RECIPIENT

Mary Edwards Walker was raised to be a freethinker. In 1855 she became the second woman in the US to earn a medical degree. She was struggling to attract patients for her private practice when the Civil War broke out. The doctor immediately tried to enlist in the Union army, but they wouldn't accept her as a medical officer. She went to Washington, DC anyway, working for free in a temporary hospital set up in the US Patent Office while organizing the Women's Relief Organization to support the families of wounded soldiers. Then Mary went straight to the front lines, volunteering in field hospitals and serving with such courage and competence that the powers that be were finally convinced. She was officially hired as the US Army's first female surgeon in 1863. The following year, her habit of crossing enemy lines to treat civilians saw her captured by Confederate forces. She spent four months in the infamous Castle Thunder Prison before being released in a swap of medical personnel. For the remainder of the war, she filled medical director posts at a hospital for female prisoners and an orphan asylum. After the war was over, President Andrew Johnson recognized Mary's distinguished service with the Medal of Honor. Out of 3,500 recipients, she was the first—and remains the only—woman honoree.

Mary's post-military career as a women's rights activist and touring health lecturer was more controversial. Professionally encumbered by traditional female attire, she became a prominent dress reformer. Her penchant for wearing male suits and top hats got her arrested on several occasions on charges of "impersonating a man." Mary also tried to vote and twice ran for federal office long before women were legally granted the right. When, in 1917, her Medal of Honor was rescinded because she had not participated in "actual combat," she defiantly proceeded to wear it every day for the rest of her life. Sixty years later, the hero's history-making medal was officially reinstated in acknowledgment of her "gallantry, self-sacrifice, patriotism, dedication, and unflinching loyalty to her country."

"It is literally impossible for one with any force of character and humanity to remain 'in the background,' when convinced by knowledge and reason, that their mission is evidently one that will result in great good."

MARY EDWARDS WALKER
SURGEON

Margaret Chase Smith

1897–1995

OFFICE WORKER • MAINE'S 1ST FEMALE US CONGRESSPERSON • POLITICAL CONSCIENCE SPARKER

On June 1, 1950, Margaret Chase Smith spoke eloquently about core US values on the Senate floor. Part of a farsighted "Declaration of Conscience," the statement made her the first Republican to go on record against the tactics of McCarthyism. In a Cold War climate of fear and suspicion, Senator Joseph McCarthy had begun a campaign to purge government, universities, and industries of people he alleged to be communist spies or Soviet sympathizers. When Margaret's repeated requests for proof were ignored, she decided it was time to publicly challenge what was swiftly becoming a "forum of hate and character assassination." Her 15-minute speech was an act of political valor, particularly because she was a freshman senator and the only woman serving in the upper house, while he was the rising star of her own party. Joe McCarthy may have dismissed Margaret and the six others who signed her statement as "Snow White and the Six Dwarfs," but she was vindicated in the end when his activities were officially censured by the Senate in 1954. Margaret not only survived her opposition to him, she came out looking like a moral beacon, one who would win three more terms for a record-making 24-year tenure.

Margaret had gotten into politics through marriage, but her long, distinguished career soon eclipsed her husband's. A barber's daughter unable to afford college, she worked in the offices of a local newspaper before marrying its owner at age 34. When he was elected to the US House of Representatives in 1936, she acted as his secretary and speech writer. After suffering a heart attack, he encouraged Margaret to take his place on the ballot for the 1940 election. She won her late husband's seat with 60% of the vote. The first woman to serve federally in both houses of Congress, Margaret spent her more than 30 years in office advocating for education, national defense, women in the military, and space exploration, while being counted among the world's most influential women.

"Those of us who shout the loudest about Americanism are all too frequently those who, by our own words and acts, ignore some of the basic principles of Americanism: the right to criticize; the right to hold unpopular beliefs; the right to protest; the right of independent thought."

MARGARET CHASE SMITH
SENATOR

Indra Nooyi

born 1955

INDIA-BORN BUSINESS STUDENT • RENOWNED STRATEGIST • VALUES CREATOR

In 2006, Indra Nooyi was named CEO of PepsiCo. She was the first woman to head the flagship American brand, and, at the time, one of only 11 female top execs in the Fortune 500. (Today there are triple that, though they still make up less than 7% overall.) Indra had been with the company since 1994, when she signed on as its chief strategist, and was later tapped to be its president and CFO. She inherited the top job at an uncertain time, with the global financial crisis looming, and had to map out a strategy to meet the challenges—would she try for morale-boosting immediate gains or equip the corporation to thrive in the long haul? The calm captain opted for the latter, charting her course with one simple, visionary principle: creating value through values. She began shifting Pepsi's portfolio away from its sugary offerings to healthier options for the whole family, giving back with childhood health initiatives, and stressing environmental sustainability as the key-stone to sustainable growth. Her tack paid off. In her 12 years at the helm, Indra upped revenue from $35 billion to $63.5 billion, keeping the company's shares steadily rising despite an international downturn in soda consumption.

Indra was a rebel kid in a conservative family. She played lead guitar in an all-girl rock band and had the audacity to pursue a Yale MBA—when still unmarried—against her mother's wishes. Known for wearing saris to corporate functions, she considers herself equal parts daughter of India and all-American businesswoman. Both her deeply traditional roots and rebellious streak have served her well in her groundbreaking career. At Pepsi, she was famous for "thinking outside the can" while ensuring the company was grounded in principles. Indra stepped down as CEO in 2018, ready to apply her sense of purpose to new projects. Besides writing a book to share what she's learned from her decades of leadership, the admired exec is dedicating herself to helping other values-driven women rise to the top.

Values make an unsinkable ship.

INDRA NOOYI
CHIEF EXECUTIVE OFFICER

Cristeta Comerford

born 1962

YOUNG FOOD LOVER • WHITE HOUSE'S 1ST FEMALE
EXECUTIVE CHEF • CULINARY DIPLOMAT

For Cristeta Comerford, the kitchen table was the heart of her childhood home in Manila. Cooking was her mother's "language of love," and the accomplished professional still considers her mom the most talented chef she's met. When her family relocated from the Philippines to Chicago in 1983, Cristeta entered the restaurant industry as a hotel "salad girl." Starting at the bottom and working her way up taught her to appreciate the importance of even small duties to the overall success of a team. She approached each step along her journey as a learning opportunity, and the diligent and passionate foodie eventually graduated from prepping Cobb salads to leading elite teams who set the menu for the world's most influential diners.

After studying French cookery in Austria and working in fine dining in Washington, DC, Cristeta was selected from among hundreds of applicants to join the White House kitchen staff as an assistant chef in 1995. Ten years later, First Lady Laura Bush promoted her to the top spot after she wowed the first couple with a specially prepared tasting menu. The first woman and first person of color to hold the executive chef position since it was created by the Kennedys in 1961, Cristeta's also the only chef in the country whose culinary briefs are top secret. After more than two decades of feeding four first families, plus foreign dignitaries, national heroes, and A-list celebs, Cristeta's become an expert at adapting her fare to suit the needs and tastes of each administration. She's made an art of state dinners, doing months of research to ensure her courses showcase the best of American cuisine while honoring guests' distinctive food cultures. Always a fan of regional, seasonal cooking, dating back to the days when she used to prepare meals using meat and produce from her grandparents' farm, today Cristeta's menus are so locally inspired, she doesn't have to go much farther than the gardens on the White House's South Lawn to source fresh herbs, vegetables, and honey straight from the hive.

"

At the end of the day, whatever you do and whatever your mission is, it's only successful because of your team.

"

CRISTETA COMERFORD
CHEF

INGENIOUSLY

"Forgive me if I don't have all the words.
Maybe I can sing it and you'll understand."

ELLA FITZGERALD
JAZZ SINGER

Emma Willard

1787–1870

SCHOOL FOUNDER • MOTHER OF WOMEN'S HIGHER ED • NURTURER OF FEMALE GENIUS

After more than a decade spent teaching women to become charming ladies worth wooing, Emma Willard became frustrated with the frivolous curricula she was forced to oversee. In an impassioned 1819 address to the New York legislature, she presented the problem with the state of women's education: "the taste of men, whatever it might happen to be, has been made into a standard for the formation of the female character." Her solution? A school that would do more than "decorate the blossom" by giving students a solid intellectual foundation in math, philosophy, history, and science. The congressmen weren't convinced, but the governor was. With his backing, plus the support of many influential wives of prominent leaders, Emma opened Troy Female Seminary in 1821. Ten years later, her campus was home to 300 girls and turning a profit through its pioneering programs. Her success saw her lecture all over the world and become a renowned authority on teaching methods and philosophies. Emma wrote history and geography textbooks filled with 3D timelines and graphic teaching aids that sold more than a million copies.

The celebrity educator had received only two years of formal schooling herself. One of 17 children in a family that supported education for both girls and boys, she'd enrolled in a local Connecticut academy at age 15. At 17, the star pupil was cordially invited to join the teaching staff there, later rising to become headmistress at Vermont's Middlebury Female Seminary. In 1814 she left to open a boarding school in her own home, based on her nephew's rigorous and well-rounded studies at the nearby Middlebury College. The Emma Willard House—a designated national landmark considered to be the birthplace of women's higher ed—is now the admissions building for the esteemed private liberal arts college. Renamed after its founder in 1895, the Emma Willard School in Troy, New York, is also still going strong, with 8,000 grads and counting. Its game-changing alumnae include everyone from suffragist Elizabeth Cady Stanton to Senator Kirsten Gillibrand.

Though well to decorate
the blossom, it is far
better to prepare for
the harvest.

EMMA WILLARD
EDUCATOR

Martha Graham

1894–1991

LATE-BLOOMING DANCER • TECHNIQUE INVENTOR •
"MOTHER OF MODERN DANCE"

Martha Graham was the most influential dancer of the 20th century, almost single-handedly transforming her craft into a distinctly modern art. The Pennsylvania doctor's daughter didn't discover dance until she was 17, but was hooked by the very first performance she attended—a production by the innovative Ruth St. Denis at an LA opera house. When Ruth opened a school, Martha eagerly enrolled. She stayed on as a teacher before going East to pursue her own artistic vision—a new type of dance that would strip away its more "decorative" elements and concentrate on embodying the raw core of human experience. In 1926, she founded a Manhattan dance company and school as an incubator for her vision. It didn't take long for her experimental techniques to get noticed. Set against the fluid and floating beauty of classical ballet, Martha's moves were stark, full of tension and release. She wanted each moment and motion to surge with vitality and meaning.

Martha's repertoire of 181 ballets was inspired by epic myths, US history, and folk traditions—from Native American ceremonies to ragtime music. Her hopeful 1944 classic, *Appalachian Spring*, is laced with square dancing patterns staged around a simple set with Shaker furniture. Often driven by powerful female protagonists, her performances offered imaginative interpretations of great women, from Joan of Arc to Emily Dickinson. Though she maintained creative control over the whole of her productions, she was also a consummate collaborator, including with US legends like composer Aaron Copeland and designer Calvin Klein. Her onstage career far outlasted that of your average ballerina. She took starring roles well into her 70s and choreographed pieces into her 90s. Recognized as a national treasure, Martha was the first dancer to perform at the White House and to earn a Presidential Medal of Freedom. Today the Martha Graham Dance Company is the country's oldest and most revered. But, true to their founder's spirit, they continue to evolve their craft with freedom, honesty, and ingenuity.

"

Make the moment important, vital and worth living. Do not let it slip away unnoticed and unused.

"

MARTHA GRAHAM
CHOREOGRAPHER

Mary Blair

1911–1978

PAINTER, DESIGNER & ART DIRECTOR • EARLY DISNEY MUSE • SORCERESS OF COLOR

When Walt Disney needed someone to design his "It's a Small World" attraction—a pavilion originally commissioned for UNICEF at the 1964 New York World's Fair—he called one of his favorite Imagineers out of retirement. A nationally recognized watercolor painter, Mary Blair reluctantly left the ranks of starving artists to join his team in 1940. Though she arrived with a visual sophistication that benefited from her fine arts training, her on-the-job experience was essential to drawing out the unique flair that made her illustrations so influential. After hiring her as an entry-level sketcher, Walt handpicked Mary to accompany him and a band of fellow artists on a 3-month research trip to South America. He had two projects in the works to promote cultural exchange and wanted his animators to begin painting from life. The more Mary immersed herself in the colors and rhythms of South America, the more her brush came alive. She returned home with not only the groundbreaking concept art for Walt's films but also a signature style.

While many animators were aiming for "naturalistic" depictions of settings, characters, and movements, Mary's approach was unapologetically expressionistic. Her witty and imaginative sketches playfully experimented with scale, dimension, and unpredictable color palettes. Her vivid touch can be seen in a series of early Disney classics, including *Cinderella, Alice in Wonderland*, and *Peter Pan*. After going freelance in 1953, Mary designed everything from advertisements to note cards and mammoth murals. She illustrated a host of Little Golden Books and oversaw the set design for Radio City Music Hall's holiday spectaculars. "It's a Small World" became her pet project and masterpiece. Starting with the premise "every child is all children," Mary and her team dreamt up a vibrant mini-tour of 26 countries populated with singing and dancing animatronic dolls. Today, the World's Fair hit remains a favorite ride at Disney theme parks, from Florida to Tokyo, while a new generation of Imagineers turns to Mary's dazzling concept art for fresh inspiration.

> "
> You get an education
> in school and in college.
> And then you start to
> work, and that's when
> you learn!
> "

MARY BLAIR
ANIMATOR

Margaret Hamilton

born 1936

COMPUTER SCIENCE PIONEER • "SOFTWARE ENGINEERING" COINER •
SAVIOR OF THE APOLLO 11 MISSION

The year 2019 marked the 50th anniversary of the first moon landing. Commemorations revealed new dimensions of the milestone mission that hadn't gotten much press before, including some of its instrumental unsung women, like Margaret Hamilton. In many ways, her contributions to the Apollo program marked as great a leap for humankind as that initial step on the lunar surface. Margaret got involved with computer science before it was an academic field. The young mathematician didn't mind learning on the job and developed a passion for doing things that had never been done. After working on an MIT project to develop weather-predicting software, Margaret was hired to head a team of 100 that created NASA's Apollo Flight Guidance Computer Software Collection. Her rigorous and creative approach to anticipating problems was so effective there were zero software bugs during any crewed Apollo mission.

Today, it's hard to imagine the differences in method and scale that Margaret had to contend with. Computers were room-sized and had no screens. Code was written on paper and translated onto punch cards to feed into the machine or manufactured into ropes of copper wire for in-flight instructions. The spacecrafts carried 72 kilobytes of computer memory—about a million times less than the storage space on your average smartphone. Yet the principles she established laid the groundwork for a radically new engineering discipline. When her young daughter managed to crash the whole system by hitting one wrong button, Margaret realized she had to account for failures in "peopleware." That extra programming proved essential in the dramatic final moments before Neil Armstrong first touched down on the moon. The landing module began flashing emergency warning signals during their approach, but Margaret's error detection and recovery mechanisms kicked in, accurately diagnosing and compensating for a malfunction in the hardware. Mission Control had such faith in Margaret, they gave the astronauts the historic green light to proceed. She would go on innovating in her field, founding two software companies that applied her lessons from Apollo to develop programming languages for complex systems.

There was no choice but to be pioneers; no time to be beginners.

MARGARET HAMILTON
SOFTWARE ENGINEER

Nonny de la Peña

born 1962

JOURNALIST • TECH COMPANY FOUNDER & CEO •
"GODMOTHER OF VIRTUAL REALITY"

We often think of virtual reality as the future of marketing, gaming, and entertainment. Nonny de la Peña, an early VR advocate and maker, has always thought about the technology's potential in a different light—as an "empathy machine," a tool for genuinely understanding the realities of others. Now a founder/CEO of a pioneering virtual and augmented reality studio, Nonny came to the industry through a distinguished career in journalism. An intern had come back in tears from a research trip for a 2010 article. Her footage recorded an LA food bank worker shouting "there's too many people!" with desperate frustration as one man waiting in the enormous line collapses into a diabetic coma because his blood sugar had gotten too low. Nonny knew that if she could allow people to experience this scene as her intern had, they'd understand the story not just with their minds but with their entire bodies. She debuted *Hunger in LA* at the 2012 Sundance Film Festival. Even though it was presented via a duct-taped headset with rudimentary graphics, the world's first VR film fueled the visceral reactions she was looking for. The president of the World Economic Forum took notice, commissioning her to design a piece about the Syrian refugee crisis, and the projects have kept coming.

Featured on news platforms, at conventions, and in top-flight museums, Nonny's VR inventions—which she's dubbed "immersive journalism"—are generating powerful new ways to put people on the scene. Distilling complex, urgent issues into graspable experiences, her team at Emblematic has taken viewers to the base of melting glaciers, put them in solitary confinement, and asked them to traverse war-torn streets. A stickler for journalistic integrity, Nonny's jumping-off point for every project is rigorous documentary, combining real footage with painstaking digital reconstructions. Her next big mission? Making VR more accessible so that everyone has the chance to not only be transported to fantastic imaginary worlds but also engage more meaningfully in our own.

What if I could present you a story that you would remember with your entire body and not just your mind?

NONNY DE LA PEÑA
VIRTUAL REALITY INNOVATOR

PASSIONATELY

"My mission in life is not merely to survive,
but to thrive; and to do so
with some passion, some compassion,
some humor, and some style."

MAYA ANGELOU
MEMOIRIST

Emma Lazarus

1849–1887

NOTED AUTHOR • ADVOCATE FOR IMMIGRANTS & REFUGEES • VOICE OF THE STATUE OF LIBERTY

Poet Emma Lazarus was famous in her day, but it certainly wasn't for her now iconic sonnet, enshrined on the pedestal of New York Harbor's beloved Lady Liberty. Affluent and educated, Emma had begun composing and translating poems as a teen. The author already had two acclaimed collections of poetry, a novel, and a play under her belt by the time she took an interest in the contemporary social issues that would dominate her later work. Born into a prosperous fourth-generation Jewish American household, Emma did not initially feel much connection to New York's sizable population of poor Jewish immigrants. Yet when a member of her inner intellectual circle filled her in on the plight of Jewish refugees barely escaping persecution in Russia, her artistic conscience was pricked. She visited a refugee camp and wrote such an affecting article about the abysmal conditions she witnessed that a few days later a nearby factory offered employment to the camp's downtrodden residents.

Besides using her pen in the service of immigrants, Emma volunteered to teach them English, worked at the Hebrew Immigrant Aid Society, and ran her own charitable fund. When, in 1883, she was asked to write a poem as part of a fundraiser to cover the costs of the pedestal at the base of the Statue of Liberty, she only agreed for the sake of amplifying her pet cause. "The New Colossus" was an impassioned call for the US to open its arms to the "huddled masses yearning to breathe free," but it didn't make much of an impression at the time. The poem was auctioned off cheaply to an unknown buyer and didn't resurface until a friend privately commissioned a pedestal plaque with the poem engraved on it as a tribute to the late author in 1903. Today, Emma's magnum opus contains some of the only lines of poetry still widely known by heart. Whether in earnest or parody, her words have become a staple of modern-day public debates surrounding the promise and shortcomings of this melting-pot nation.

New aims, new interests rise with each new sun.

EMMA LAZARUS
POET

Gloria Vanderbilt

1924–2019

SOCIALITE & FASHION ICON • MODEL, ACTOR, PAINTER, WRITER • MOTHER OF DESIGNER DENIM

Gloria Vanderbilt had an enormous appetite for life. Moving from one passion project to the next, she pursued tandem careers as a model, actor, poet, painter, memoirist, novelist, designer, and fashion mogul by the time she passed away at 95. Whatever the railroad heiress did, she knew it would be in the limelight. Her idyllic baby pictures were splashed on the pages of *Vogue*, but her father died soon after her birth. At 10, she became tabloid fodder as the centerpiece of a bitter 1934 custody battle. After hours of salacious courtroom testimonies about her widowed mother's lax lifestyle, her aunt won the suit. Determined to live down the epitaph "poor little rich girl," Gloria set out to write her own headlines. If her famous name was a magnet for publicity, she might as well promote her own agenda instead of the paparazzi's.

After modeling for top magazines as a teen, Gloria found her artistic muse. Her colorful canvases would eventually inspire textile and stationery designs. In the 1970s, the high-fashion icon decided to go into the ready-to-wear jeans business. At the time, denim was stiff workwear mostly worn by men. Gloria made it a glamorous essential of the American woman's wardrobe by coming out with her signature line of dark, fitted jeans that "really hug your derrière." Emblazoning her name across the back pocket of every pair, and even modeling for her own ads, Gloria built a multimillion-dollar fashion empire. In the last chapter of her life, that illustrious name would also grace many a book cover. Her best-selling memoirs include a romantic history of her four marriages—plus high-profile trysts with the likes of Frank Sinatra, Howard Hughes, and Marlon Brando. Another shared a candid account of her grieving process after losing a son to suicide. Still creating into her 90s, Gloria's last book of heartfelt and hard-won wisdom was coauthored with her son, network news anchor Anderson Cooper.

"

I'm in love with beauty
and things and people
and love and being
in love, and those things
I think, on the inside,
show on the outside.

"

GLORIA VANDERBILT
FASHION DESIGNER

Ruth E. Carter

born 1960

**THEATER BUFF • 1ST BLACK WOMAN TO WIN
A COSTUME DESIGN OSCAR • WARDROBE STORYTELLER**

Growing up, Ruth E. Carter assumed that art was just a hobby, something that inner-city kids dallied at in after-school programs but not a real vocation. She started college as a special ed major but found that theater arts had a magnetic draw she couldn't ignore. By the time she graduated, the young "student of her passion" had become Hampton University's go-to costume designer. After unpaid internships and a gig as a lowly stitcher for an opera house, Ruth moved to LA to ply her craft. Working her way from dresser to foreperson of the costume shop with the newly built Los Angeles Theatre Center, she caught the eye of Hollywood movers and shakers when she volunteered as pro bono costume designer for a dance production directed by groundbreaking choreographer Otis Sallid. Then, one day she got a life-changing call from director Spike Lee. He invited her out of her theatrical comfort zone to work on his 1988 film *School Daze*. More than a dozen collaborations later, she still credits Spike with giving her the freedom to become an artist and the self-belief to become a leader.

Since then, Ruth has proven time and again how costumes make the character. Her penchant for research and meticulous attention to detail have made her a sought-after head designer, known for authentically outfitting period-piece ensembles in landmark films like *Malcom X*, *Amistad*, *Selma*, and *The Butler*. Her historic 2019 Oscar win for the Marvel superhero film *Black Panther* made her a household name. Fashioning the hundreds of costumes necessary for the blockbuster was an epic undertaking requiring two teams and warehouses. With its sci-fi setting in the imaginary sub-Saharan nation of Wakanda, the project challenged Ruth to invent her own Afro-futuristic aesthetic. Now one of film's most recognizable below-the-line names, the ingenious costumer is using her well-earned fame to usher in a golden age of inclusivity and individual expression in the industry.

"Be a student of your passion."

RUTH E. CARTER
COSTUME DESIGNER

Jill Ellis

born 1966

BACK-TO-BACK WORLD CUP CHAMP • US SOCCER'S WINNINGEST COACH • ADRENALINE-FUELED TACTICIAN

Jill Ellis was born in England, the home of football. The Manchester United fan spent years on the sidelines watching her father coach, but there were no organized leagues for girls. It wasn't until she moved to the US at 16 that she finally got in the game herself. After a standout NCAA career as a striker at William & Mary, she decided to follow in her dad's footsteps, putting in time at every level of soccer in the US, from club to college to international. When she was named head coach of the US Women's National Team, the 2015 FIFA World Cup was in her sights—a tournament they'd not won since 1999. The US was ranked #1, but she knew that fulfilling expectations meant prepping her players to cope with curveballs. She even took them to a tournament in Brazil where they met with extreme heat, waterlogged pitches, and 10,000 fans booing as a lesson in adversity. Her players rose to the challenge, taking home the US's third world title.

Just a year later, the team had their worst result in a major tournament. They went into the 2016 Olympics as favorites but were knocked out in the quarterfinals. The underperformance left Jill with a mounting raft of critics that reached all the way into her own locker room. She didn't fold under the pressure. Instead, the coach took it as a reminder that even successful teams need to keep evolving. From then on, no player was guaranteed a spot in her starting lineup, no matter how veteran. Jill's controversial stance strengthened the bonds between her players, who couldn't settle into comfortable cliques. Her never-satisfied mentality saw the US National Team come back with a vengeance, dominating the 2019 World Cup with an unbeaten scorecard, record number of goals, and millions of viewers. Soon after, Jill decided to walk away on top. As one of two coaches in history to win two FIFA titles, she retired with a 106-7-19 record and an amazing legacy of raising the global profile of women's sports.

"It's not about the medals.
It's not about the matches.
It's about the moments.
It's those moments that
make you feel alive."

JILL ELLIS
SOCCER COACH

Hilary Hutcheson

born 1978

EXPERT GUIDE • BACKCOUNTRY FUN-FINDER • "WILD FEMINIST" & CLIMATE ACTIVIST

Hilary Hutcheson has a simple mantra: have a good time. Raised at the foot of Glacier National Park by parents who worked for the National Park Service, she spent her childhood hiking snowy passes and rafting whitewater rapids. When she and her sister discovered a dusty cache of flies in a neighbor's shed, it didn't take long for them to get hooked on another wilderness hobby. Hilary became Glacier Anglers' first female guide as a teenager. New clients would sometimes look dubiously at their petite German Japanese expedition leader, but after she showed them a rip-roaring good time, they'd come back specifically requesting her. She landed a broadcasting job with a Portland TV station straight out of college. But five years into her journalism career, Hilary decided it was time to add more play into her work. She went back to her Montana hometown, ready to take up her rod again. But this time, she wanted to do it on her own eco-friendly terms.

Hilary had become increasingly aware that having a good time depends on protecting the natural resources that give us pleasure. If rivers are polluted or going dry, that pretty much shuts the party down. As a boss, she could be an industry and environmental leader, putting conservation at the heart of all her work and fun. Hilary's adventurous ventures include a fly and supply shop, a marketing firm for outdoorsy types, and a network fly-fishing program, *Trout TV*, which she's cohosted since 2011. Besides being a brand ambassador for some of the biggest names in gear—Patagonia, Yeti, Orvis—she's a vocal envoy for protecting public lands, transitioning to clean energy, and combating the effects of climate change. The professional thrill-seeker also continues to conduct float trips for aspiring anglers on the Flathead and Salmon Rivers. She knows that, no matter a person's convictions, if you give them an unforgettable experience, they're more likely to walk away as staunch defenders of those sacred wild places where we live and play.

> A lot of people say you should separate your work and play, but I think that's the only way I get to play so hard.

HILARY HUTCHESON
FLY-FISHER

PROFOUNDLY

"I am as much a part of the universe
as any speck of stardust."

MAE JEMISON
ASTRONAUT

Bridget "Biddy" Mason

1818–1891

NURSE & MIDWIFE • SELF-MADE MILLIONAIRE • FAITHFUL PHILANTHROPIST

Biddy Mason was born into slavery. When she died, she was one of the wealthiest women in Los Angeles. At that time, her real estate investments were worth $300,000—about $8 million by today's standards. For 10 years, Biddy saved her $2.50-per-week earnings as a midwife to buy land. Little did she know, the properties she started acquiring for $250 a pop would one day be worth a fortune. As one of the first African American women to own property, she firmly believed that her personal investments should also pay dividends to her community. Her oft-repeated philosophy—"An open hand is blessed, for it gives in abundance even as it receives"—has been passed down through the generations as a family motto. Besides making frequent visits to prison inmates, risking her life to treat victims of a smallpox epidemic, and steadfastly catering to those in need, Biddy opened her own home as an orphanage and day care center for working mothers. She would go on to establish an elementary school for African American children and the First African Methodist Episcopal Church in downtown LA.

Originally from Mississippi, Biddy was steered west when her master joined a 300-wagon caravan to Utah. She was forced to walk thousands of miles, serving as a cook and midwife while herding her three young daughters and the livestock. But the grueling migration held a ray of hope. Biddy discovered that slavery was illegal in their ultimate destination, the state of California. Though she had been barred from learning to read or write, she managed to bring her master to court in 1856. He bribed her lawyer not to show, but she won the suit anyway, gaining freedom for herself plus 13 other slaves. Never granted a surname, after the trial Biddy chose her own. She soon made "Mason" synonymous with great savvy, generosity, and compassion. Today that name graces an LA park on the land she once donated to build her church and a foundation established by its current congregants to honor her charitable vision.

> **"**
>
> If you hold your hand
> closed, nothing good
> can come in.
>
> **"**

BIDDY MASON
REAL ESTATE ENTREPRENEUR

Anna Mary Robertson Moses

1860–1961

FARMER • ENTERPRISING CRAFTSPERSON • LATE-BREAKING CULTURAL SENSATION

Anna Mary Robertson Moses didn't start painting until her late 70s. She spent those years that most devote to retirement creating 1,500 works that would make her one of the best-known folk artists of the 20th century—the much beloved Grandma Moses. Born on a farm and helping run one for most of her life, Anna was in the habit of keeping busy. She began working at a neighboring farm by age 12, eventually settling with her husband on one of her own in Virginia's Shenandoah Valley and later in upstate New York. Besides raising their children and tending to the house and farm, Anna sold a variety of homemade foods to boost the family's income. Amid the intense demands of rural life, she also found time for creative expression. As a child, she would draw on old newsprint, pressing berries to add splashes of color. As an adult, she developed a talent for making colorful quilts and needlework pictures according to her own intricate patterns. When arthritis made embroidery nearly impossible, Anna went looking for a new medium. She exchanged her needle for a brush, using whatever scraps she could find—discarded fireboard, leftover tubs of enamel—to compose her first paintings.

The 78-year-old artist was selling her charming canvases alongside her prize-winning pickles at county fairs when a fine art collector saw her works in a local pharmacy's window display and bought the whole lot. In 1939 he helped Anna secure her first museum show—an exhibit to showcase unknown talents at New York City's Museum of Modern Art. Her inspirational never-too-late-to-shine story combined with her rosy, nostalgic representations of America's pastoral past made her paintings resonate beyond elite galleries. They're still widely reproduced on stationery and home decor. For Anna, each painting evoked a cherished memory—making apple butter and harvesting pumpkins, cozy neighborhood gatherings in farmhouse kitchens and country weddings under leafy arbors. Grandma Moses died at 101, happy she'd put in "a good day's work," as a profound example of making the best out of what life has to offer.

Life is what we make it, always has been, always will be.

GRANDMA MOSES
FOLK ARTIST

Toni Morrison

PROFESSOR • 1ST AFRICAN AMERICAN NOBEL PRIZE
IN LITERATURE WINNER • NATIONAL TREASURE

Toni Morrison was born in a working-class Ohio steel town during the darkest days of the Great Depression. Her father took as many factory jobs as he could to provide his daughter with a better life. Yet Toni's childhood was filled with inspiration. It was the humble yet rich foundation for her towering, world-moving art. Lorain's inhabitants were a vibrant and tolerant mix of new arrivals—Eastern European and Mexican immigrants along with African Americans relocated to the North. There was no such thing as a "black neighborhood"; everyone lived and played together. Her home was crammed with storytellers whose idioms were rooted in religion, black folklore, and Southern life. The young Toni was deeply impressed by the vividness and musicality of their language. Channeling these under-acknowledged American stories and cultures would become her life's work.

But the would-be author didn't pick up a pen until she herself entered the publishing industry in 1965. Recently divorced, Toni secretly spent the evenings after her young sons went to bed slipping into the safe space of writing. Following her own editorial advice—"If you find a book you really want to read, but it hasn't been written yet, then you must write it"—she spent five years completing her first slim novel, *The Bluest Eye*, based on a classmate trained to judge herself according to white standards of beauty. Her literary breakthrough came with the 1987 Pulitzer-Prize-winning *Beloved,* a haunting take on the true story of an escaped slave who tried to kill herself and her children rather than return to the plantation. These and other Toni classics have become mainstays of school reading lists as lyrical entrées to unresolved elements of our collective past. Besides writing books, Toni edited and taught them. As an editor, she promoted excellent black authors who weren't getting their due. As a longtime educator who was the first African American endowed chair at an Ivy League school, she empowered students to learn the art of empowering others.

"

Your life is already artful—waiting, just waiting, for you to make it art.

"

TONI MORRISON
AUTHOR

Ann Bancroft

born 1955

RECORD-MAKING ADVENTURER • 1ST WOMAN TO REACH BOTH POLES • GLOBAL WILDERNESS EDUCATOR

The young Ann Bancroft never felt comfortable within classroom walls. Struggling with an undiagnosed learning disability in an era before special education, she became a devoted student of the great outdoors. Her rural Minnesota home offered ample opportunities for learning, like canoe trips with her family or winter camping in a neighbor's backyard. When Ann's dyslexia was finally recognized, it motivated her to go into education. She was teaching phys ed when her application to join the 1986 Steger International Polar Expedition got a surprising green light. Crossing more than 1,000 miles of ice, Ann became the first woman to reach the North Pole by foot and dogsled. Lauded as one of the world's preeminent explorers, she went on to headline other daring snow adventures—leading the first groups of women to cross Greenland and reach the South Pole on skis—while promoting outdoors and environmental curricula to a global classroom of five million.

In 2001, the intrepid educator got an unexpected lesson in moral courage. She and Norwegian collaborator Liv Arnesen had spent three years planning, training, and fundraising for an expedition that would make them the first women to cross Antarctica. After a grueling 94-day trek in subzero temperatures, hauling 250-pound sleds, they'd traversed the 1,717 miles of the continent's landmass. Liv had almost slipped down a crevasse, Ann had torn a shoulder muscle, but now they faced their greatest "moment of truth"—deciding whether to continue over the 400 miles of ice shelf left to reach their ultimate goal. The Antarctic summer was about to end, heralding nonstop blizzards and darkness. Continuing would not only risk their lives but those of their crew and rescuers. Ann's iron will was telling her to go on no matter what, but she thought of their millions of kid followers and knew it was important to make the right choice—one that didn't put her personal ambition first. She found the mettle to come up short. Today, the explorer continues to harness her adventurous spirit to inspire young seekers on their journeys.

"

I'm always wondering, how will I act at my moment of truth?

"

ANN BANCROFT
EXPLORER

Katie Bouman

born 1989

COMPUTATIONAL IMAGING PRODIGY • STEM PROF • BLACK HOLE "SEER"

Black holes—one of the most mysterious phenomena in our universe and yet one of the most fundamental—are thought to be the pulsing hearts at the center of most galaxies. Their gravitational pull is so strong that nothing can escape, not even light, which means there's no way to "see" them aside from the shadows they cast onto the glowing hot discs of dust and gas presumed to whir around their edges. They're so dense and distant that trying to capture an image of one is like spotting an orange on the Moon with your naked eye. Nonetheless, a daring team of 200 international researchers decided to attempt the impossible, by synchronizing a network of radio telescopes that spanned the entire Earth. But how could they possibly piece together the scant patchwork of noisy data collected to create a comprehensible picture? Enter computational imaging whiz Katie Bouman. The Indiana native had no background in physics or astronomy when she joined the Event Horizon Telescope project in 2013. But she did have an uncanny knack for finding ways to see and measure the invisible.

As an MIT grad student and postdoc, Katie helped forge the code that could render an image from thousands of bytes of data. At her insistence, the crew spent two years testing and refining the algorithm to ensure they hadn't designed it to construct the picture they expected to see. She knew that, for the results to be scientifically valid, they had to leave open the possibility that they'd reveal a "giant elephant" instead of a dark sphere. Finally, the mountain of data they were waiting for—gleaned from a galaxy 54 million light-years away—arrived, manually shipped on half a ton of hard drives. The 29-year-old Katie was amazed to see a hazy orange ring immediately come into view. It was the world's first visualization of a black hole—exactly as Albert Einstein had predicted it would look more than 100 years earlier. Now a Caltech professor, Katie's excited for the Event Horizon Telescope's new target: imaging the 4-million-solar-mass black hole in the middle of our own Milky Way.

"

Is it possible to see something that, by definition, is impossible to see?

"

KATIE BOUMAN
COMPUTER SCIENTIST

PURPOSELY

"Every moment is an organizing opportunity, every person a potential activist, every minute a chance to change the world."

DOLORES HUERTA
LABOR LEADER

Jovita Idár

1885–1946

TEACHER TURNED CAMPAIGNER • NEWSPAPER EDITOR & PUBLISHER • WORKING WOMAN FOR EQUALITY

Jovita Idár was born into a large family with a big purpose—civil rights for Mexican Americans. Disturbed by escalating violence and discrimination aimed at Texas's Chicano residents, her father founded a Spanish-language newspaper in Laredo as a bullhorn for advocacy. Jovita trained as a teacher, taking up her first post in 1904, but soon grew so disillusioned with the public school system's segregation and neglect of Mexican American students that she resigned in protest. Convinced she could better serve her pupils outside the classroom, Jovita joined her father and two brothers on the staff of *La Crónica*. As a reporter and columnist, she called out injustices related to subpar education, housing, and working conditions. She argued for bilingual teaching and cultural preservation, helping to convene the First Mexican Congress that brought together activists from both sides of the Rio Grande.

Jovita also took a stand as an unapologetic feminist. In 1911, she published the bold editorial "We Must Work," urging women to brush aside unworthy critics and backward social conventions to pursue work that would secure their financial independence and benefit society. That same year, she organized those "honorable working women" into the League of Mexican Women to back suffrage, tackle sexism, and establish free educational programs to lift up the poorest children in their communities. An ardent supporter of the Mexican Revolution, Jovita crossed the border to nurse soldiers fighting for democracy. Recruited to write for *El Progreso* upon her return, Jovita's outspoken opposition to the 1914 US occupation of Veracruz saw the Texas Rangers march on the paper's offices. She put her body on the line to personally bar the entrance, but the champion of free press could only hold them off so long. They returned the next day and destroyed the printing operations. Undeterred, she took over running *La Crónica* after her father passed away before moving to San Antonio with her husband. There, Jovita kept at her causes, editing a Methodist Church periodical, volunteering as a translator for Spanish-speaking hospital patients, and establishing a free kindergarten.

A person dedicated to certain jobs or tasks does not have time to be bothered by useless or damaging things.

JOVITA IDÁR
JOURNALIST

Pleasant Rowland

born 1941

LANGUAGE ARTS EDUCATOR • PHILANTHROPIST • ENTREPRENEUR IN THE "GIRL BUSINESS"

When Pleasant Rowland launched her best-known brainchild—the American Girl brand—in 1986, she wasn't trying get into the toy or doll or book business. She was inventing the "girl business," a company that took its young audience seriously and based commercial decisions around catering to their unmet needs. The mission came to the former elementary school teacher—who'd already made her name as a creator of popular textbooks and innovative reading programs—during a search for meaningful presents for her nieces. The toy store aisles were full of slick, shiny, neon stuff. She wanted something subtler, more thought-provoking, and creative, something they'd treasure and pass on to their own kids. A fateful trip to Colonial Williamsburg sparked an idea. Why not create a line of top-quality dolls paired with their own book series to help history come alive for today's girls? The concept was so obvious to her that she was surprised when no one else believed it would fly. She got it off the ground by trusting her gut. Acting as her own "one-person focus group," she let her 8-year-old and favorite-auntie selves steer product development. If she adored it, she knew she could find an audience that would, too.

Going against the grain of the toy industry meant making a lot of seemingly counterintuitive decisions, like not putting product in stores and advertising solely via direct mail to allow for long-form stories. When Hollywood came knocking for movie rights, she politely declined to protect the brand's long-haul vision. It has indeed stood the test of time. Launching with three dolls from colonial times to WWII, Pleasant pulled in more than $100 million in sales her very first season. As the offerings have grown more historically diverse, American Girl dolls have become second only to Barbie in the US market. Since selling her business to Mattel in 1998 for $700 million, the Pleasant Company founder has continued following her heart to new missions. Today, she's a high-impact philanthropist specializing in upping literacy, preserving history, and supporting the arts.

"Come from a place of heart. Come from a place of mission. There will be people out there who will love it and admire it if you love it and admire it."

PLEASANT ROWLAND
EDUCATIONAL TOY INNOVATOR

Dolly Parton

born 1946

MUSICIAN, ACTOR, AUTHOR, PRODUCER • BUSINESS MOGUL •
CHAMPION OF CHILDHOOD LITERACY

Born into a twig cradle in rural Appalachia and hustling her way to international superstardom, Dolly Parton's is the ultimate American "rags to rhinestones" story. One of twelve kids in a poor farming family, the down-home prodigy discovered her purpose early. She started performing professionally at age 10, made her Grand Ole Opry debut at 13, and hightailed it to Nashville after high school graduation to make good on her calling. After stealing hearts on the small screen, dueting with the pompadoured namesake of the long-running *Porter Wagoner Show*, Dolly struck out on her own. Since then, she's cut some impressive records: a Country Music Hall-of-Famer widely recognized as one of the genre's most important singer-songwriters; a 9-time Grammy winner, including the Lifetime Achievement Award; a hit-maker with classics like "Jolene" and "I Will Always Love You" that continue to inspire chart-topping covers; a savvy businesswoman who wisely retained the rights to all her songs; an entrepreneur with her own Smoky Mountain theme park that brings thrills to three million visitors a year.

She may be famous for teased wigs, high-heeled boots, and waist-cinching, bust-accentuating getups, but Dolly is also known for the sincere, unpretentious substance behind her trademark style. In 1980, the "Backwoods Barbie" became a feminist icon after starring in and writing the #1 title track for the film *9 to 5*. The landmark revenge comedy aimed at sexist bosses also got a timely Broadway reboot in a musical entirely composed by Dolly. In 1995, she earned another nickname—"the Book Lady." Dolly dreamt up Imagination Library in honor of her father, who never learned to read or write. The visionary program gives kids a book each month from birth to age five, specially delivered to their homes in a package with their name on it. A much-needed boon to early childhood education, her free library has spread to all 50 states plus four countries, delivering more than 100 million horizon-expanding books to date. This big dreamer has now set her sights on reaching the one-billion-book mark.

Find out who you are and do it on purpose.

DOLLY PARTON
SINGER-SONGWRITER

Beth Robinette

born 1987

THEATER GEEK • RANCHER & HOLISTIC LAND MANAGER • COWGIRL EDUCATOR

Beth Robinette grew up on an 800-acre ranch west of Spokane, Washington, dreaming of a career on Broadway. Her college cafeteria was a wake-up call. Once she got outside the bubble of her bucolic upbringing—working intimately with nature, eating home-cooked meals made with produce raised or grown by her family—she suddenly realized that her future lay much closer to home. Confronted with the industrialized food systems that come with heavy environmental tolls and compromise local communities' abilities to feed themselves, Beth came to see that her small family business was a genuine opportunity to sow seeds of change. She returned to Lazy R Ranch with a degree in sustainable agriculture, ready to raise premium grass-fed beef alongside her father under the eco-aware slogan: "We ranch like your future depends on it."

A fourth-generation rancher, Beth's also part of the changing face of agriculture. The recent influx of women isn't just stepping into men's boots, they're changing the profession to reconnect with the land and reshape our foodscapes. Beth's steering the herd by helping to bring ladies into the fold. In 2017, she cofounded New Cowgirl Camp, a "rhinestone-free zone" that offers a crash course in animal husbandry and holistic land management. Though cattle have gotten a bad rap as drivers of climate change, Beth believes her style of ranching can be part of the solution. At Lazy R, she's proven that better livestock starts with enhanced ecosystems—pastures teeming with life that can sequester carbon, retain water, and encourage resilience. Besides running her own farm, Beth is actively rewiring her state's food systems with LINC Foods, a cooperative hub that connects local farmers to commercial customers. As she continues to roll out projects and gain prominence—including a statewide "Farmer of the Year" cred in 2018, her core duties remain the same: long, solitary hours mending fences, choreographing grazing, and counting grass species. Whether changing the demographics of her profession, empowering regional producers, or cultivating robust ecosystems, Beth's purposeful work is boosting diversity and sustainability.

If you desire diversity, you have to create conditions for diversity to thrive.

BETH ROBINETTE
RANCHER

Emily Núñez Cavness

born 1989

MILITARY KID • US ARMY LIEUTENANT • PURPOSE-FILLED REPURPOSER

The question of how to turn the discarded into something beautifully beneficial sparked Emily Núñez Cavness's imagination one fateful day as she sat listening to a lecture by a visiting social entrepreneur. Before the talk even wrapped, the Middlebury College senior had marshaled a business plan to convert military surplus into stylish, American-made accessories. The daughter of a lifelong Army officer, she'd grown up surrounded by soldiers, calling West Point home and eating Thanksgiving dinners in bustling mess halls. She wanted to serve, too, so she enlisted in the Reserve Officer Training Program. As Middlebury College's only ROTC cadet, she soon became a de facto military ambassador in a student community where many had never met someone in the service. Galvanized by the idea of social entrepreneurship, she spotted a chance to expand her bridge-building mission with a company run by and for veterans that would reduce waste while encouraging meaningful connections between military and civilian populations. She would turn "swords into plowshares." In 2013, Emily and her sister/cofounder, Betsy, launched Sword & Plough with a Kickstarter crowdfunding campaign that raised 15 times their $20,000 goal. They were swamped with 1,500 orders to fill right as Emily learned she was being deployed to Afghanistan. She honorably performed both duties—CEO of a startup and first female intelligence office for the 10th Special Forces Group.

After joining the inaugural class of women to enter the US Army's 5-month Ranger Training Assessment Course, Emily retired from the military to run her Certified B Corp full-time. Determined to create opportunities for fellow vets, Sword & Plough routes 10% of all profits to veterans' initiatives. Veterans have also been drafted into every department, from design and manufacture to sales, fulfillment, and even modeling. Thus far, they've salvaged more than 40,000 pounds of surplus, including challenging materials like aircraft insulation. As the cofounder of a company that continues to notch up accolades for principled innovation, Emily's stepping up as a general for quadruple bottom-line businesses driven by people, planet, profits, and purpose.

> **"What in my life is sometimes discarded that could be harnessed into something beautiful with a powerful mission?"**

EMILY NÚÑEZ CAVNESS
SOCIAL ENTREPRENEUR

RESOURCEFULLY

"Champions adjust."

BILLIE JEAN KING
TENNIS LEGEND

Annie Jump Cannon

1863–1941

DELAWARE SENATOR'S DAUGHTER • HARVARD "CALCULATOR" • "CENSUS TAKER OF THE STARS"

In 1901, Annie Jump Cannon painstakingly analyzed the photographic spectra of hundreds of thousands of stars to devise her own system of classification, based on surface temperatures. It was officially adopted as the standard by the International Astronomical Union in 1922 and is still, with minor modifications, in use today. Though she'd been a science buff ever since her mother taught her the constellations, even earning a degree in physics at a time when few women attended college, Annie's storied career in astronomy almost didn't happen. In fact, after graduating at the top of her class from Wellesley, she went back to her childhood home for nearly a decade. Then a bout of scarlet fever that rendered her nearly deaf, along with her beloved mother's passing, inspired Annie to reclaim her long-lost life scientific. She secured an assistantship with a former professor and plunged into grad work. In 1896, she was hired by Harvard Observatory director Edward Pickering as a human "calculator" for a fact-gathering mission of astronomical proportions. His all-female team was paid meager clerical wages to pour over photographic plates of star spectra and index their chemical compositions. Annie proved to be amazingly gifted at this mammoth, detail-oriented undertaking. Classifying stars at a pace of 200 a day, her personal catalogue listed more than 225,000 by the end of her career.

If Edward Pickering had initially hired women because they were better and cheaper than his bungling male grad students, the female astronomers' accomplishments eventually established them as luminaries in the field. Annie was among Harvard Observatory's shining stars. In 1911, she was named its curator of astronomical photos and later its William C. Bond Astronomer. An American Astronomical Society officer, she was the first woman to receive an honorary doctorate from Oxford and to win the National Academy of Sciences' Henry Draper Medal. An asteroid and crater on the Moon bear her name . . . all nods to Annie's invaluable contribution—providing the meticulous mountain of facts necessary to spark and corroborate theories about the mighty whole.

Each fact is a factor in the mighty whole.

ANNIE JUMP CANNON
ASTRONOMER

Martha Stewart

born 1941

RENAISSANCE WOMAN • DIVA OF DOMESTICITY • COMEBACK QUEEN

When, in 2006, Martha Stewart wrote the sage advice to cut your imperfect pies (literal and metaphorical) into wedges, her own career was an uncomfortably apt illustration of the rule. Just a year before, she'd completed a 5-month prison stint and 6-month house arrest following convictions tied to a stock trading case. The unsavory episode cost her company $1 billion and could have easily sunk her hard-earned empire. Instead, the celebrity homemaker refused to let it be the defining moment of a life marked by many proud achievements. Martha had already seen success as a model and stockbroker when she moved into the Connecticut farmhouse that would become the heart of her famous lifestyle brand. Her penchants for cooking and entertaining led to a booming catering business. When she impressed an exec at a book launch event, she left with a book deal herself. Martha's 1982 publishing debut *Entertaining* was an instant hit, jump-starting her career as a guru of gracious living. Fifteen years later, she became founder, president, and CEO of her own media and merchandising company with a series of namesake books, magazines, TV shows, and product lines. Taking it public in 1999 officially made her the US's first self-made female billionaire.

Martha's reputation for perfection may have come out dented from her run-in with the law. But, in many ways, moving past the negative to dish up an amazing comeback has made her even stronger. Going against the conventional wisdom to keep a low profile, she reemerged with her head held high and her infectious zeal intact. She confidently relaunched her flagship show and found that most of her friends, fans, employees, and business partners were still on board. Since then, she's continued to introduce magazines, book titles, and TV programs while securing historic deals to add thousands of products to her portfolio, from luxe wines to fitted sheets. Now in her 70s, Martha's garnishing her classics with a twist of surprise—like the VH1 cooking show she cohosts with rapper Snoop Dogg—giving us a recipe for living well, despite imperfection.

> " "
>
> # So the pie isn't perfect?
> # Cut it in wedges.
>
> " "

MARTHA STEWART
LIFESTYLE MOGUL

Amelia Morán Ceja

born 1955

GRAPE PICKER TO VINTNER • 1ST MEXICAN AMERICAN VINEYARD PRES • ROOTS-HONORING PHILANTHROPIST

Cutting her first cluster of Merlot at age 12, Amelia Morán Ceja was immediately determined to have her own vines. When she told her father she'd run a vineyard one day, he said: "Of course you will." And she would. Amelia's dad was away working in the US for much of her childhood in Jalisco. The tiny farming village had no electricity or running water, but its bountiful love and unforgettable flavors were sturdy roots for her bright future. When her family emigrated to California in 1967, Amelia joined them in the fields on the weekends, meeting her future husband when he (unsuccessfully) tried to help her tip a heavy load into a trailer. The history and lit major was newly married with three children when she and her husband's family pooled their resources to buy their original 20-acre spread. It took five years of patient cultivation to yield a harvest and 12 more of selling grapes to other vintners before they were ready to bottle their first commercial wines in 2001. Amelia, who knew the biz from the ground up, was their pick for president. With her filling every role from marketing manager to executive chef, critics anointed Ceja Vineyard as the industry's most promising newcomer.

The first Mexican American to head a winery, Amelia's made her family-run operation into a full-bodied celebration of their heritage. Her innovative culinary pairings—tomatillo-laced oysters with Sauvignon Blanc, grilled chiles rellenos with Chardonnay—have busted the myth that wines don't mix with Latin cuisine. Having grown up with labor leaders Dolores Huerta and Cesar Chavez as her heroes (and houseguests when UFW was organizing Napa Valley), Amelia also pays tribute to her roots by protecting the rights of Mexican campesinos and raising awareness about their essential contributions to the US wine industry. She's raised hundreds of thousands of dollars for related causes and successfully lobbied for a bill banning minors from fields where pesticides are used. Today you can find the indefatigable vintner fronting her own PBS cooking series, pouring wines in the White House, and breaking ground for the vineyard's new mission-style HQ.

"

It really doesn't matter where you begin. What really matters is what you do from that point on.

"

AMELIA MORÁN CEJA
WINEMAKER

Marin Alsop

born 1956

JULLIARD-TRAINED VIOLINIST • KOUSSEVITZKY CONDUCTING
PRIZE WINNER • MUSIC'S 1ST MAESTRA

From the moment 9-year-old Marin Alsop witnessed Leonard Bernstein lift his baton and jump around the stage, she knew she wanted to be a conductor. There was only one problem: she was a girl. Her parents were both professional musicians, and they'd groomed her to follow in their footsteps. She could happily spend eight hours a day practicing her violin, but it was far more difficult to rehearse her chosen art, even with willing parents or music school buddies bribed with pizza. No conducting program would accept her without experience, and no one was willing to give her a chance. So she decided to create her own podium. Marin formed a string swing band, cutting her teeth in clubs and at weddings before convincing one of her clients to fund a full orchestra. Her innovative concert series—think gospel meets Handel's *Messiah*—finally earned her an audition for conducting school after four prior rejections. The 30-year-old student emerged as a star pupil, taken under the wing of her childhood idol, Leonard Bernstein.

After years of chasing her dream, Marin thought she'd finally gotten her foot through the front door when, in 2005, she was tapped to be the first woman music director at the Baltimore Symphony Orchestra. She'd already become the UK's first female conductor. Now as she undertook leading a major US orchestra, unflattering headlines broadcast a full-on musician revolt. Marin's openness, zeal, and vision eventually won them over, revitalizing the organization and making her a sought-after conductor, from São Paolo to Vienna to the BBC Proms. Her tempo-setting tenure has also transformed classical music. She's swapped stuffiness for an accessible, community-oriented approach that has reverberated beyond concert halls to engage adult amateurs, families, and thousands of her city's most deprived children. Describing her ultimate role as a "messenger for genius," Marin's a champion for young modern composers . . . and more female "messengers." With hundreds of experts hanging on every flick of her wrist, this master of body language reminds us how every gesture sends a message.

"Just don't give up. Just persevere. You pound and pound and pound at the front door, and then, while no one's looking, walk around the side and climb in the window."

MARIN ALSOP
CONDUCTOR

Sylvia Acevedo

born 1957

ROCKET SCIENTIST • STARTUP & NONPROFIT FOUNDER • LEADING SCOUT TURNED GIRL SCOUTS LEADER

Sylvia Acevedo has been a Stanford-educated engineer, NASA rocket scientist, Silicon Valley tech exec, software entrepreneur, award-winning education campaigner, and nonprofit leader. It's a remarkable and, given the era, unlikely career for the daughter of a Mexican immigrant raised in a hardworking family that lived paycheck to paycheck. When asked what inspired her to be a trail-blazing go-getter, she has a simple answer—she was a Girl Scout. It was a Brownie camping trip that turned Sylvia into a stargazer. Her troop leader's impromptu astronomy lesson not only set her on the path to a science badge—for which she assembled her first model rocket—but a distinguished tenure in STEM. Setting and working hard to meet her cookie sales goals gave her a sense of control and self-confidence. She also learned persistence, never walking away from a prospect until she'd heard "no" at least three times. (Sylvia still thinks the annual cookie sale is one of the best entrepreneurial and financial literacy programs around . . . and finds cracking open a box of Thin Mints to be the best kind of aromatherapy.) Most importantly, being a Scout taught her to approach challenges as a constructive problem-solver. That mindset was an asset when she was working on the Voyager mission's flyby of Jupiter or designing a state-of-the-art manufacturing facility for IBM.

From 2016 to 2020, Sylvia was at the helm of the very organization she found so formative. Founded by Juliet Gordon Low in 1912, Girl Scouts has touched the lives of nearly 60 million American girls like her—including more than half of all the US's female elected officials. As CEO, Sylvia stayed true to the original Girl Scout promise, building upon the much-loved foundation of crafts, camping, and cookies while debuting 21st-century-skills-building badges for her 1.8 million members to explore cybersecurity, robotics, and civic engagement. Her legacy? Fueling the STEM, leadership, and entrepreneurship pipelines by preparing girls with the emotional, analytical, and technical resources they need to shape the modern world.

"

If you're prepared, you can be fearless.

"

SYLVIA ACEVEDO
ENGINEER

TENACIOUSLY

"Decide what you want. Declare it to the world.
See yourself winning. And remember that
if you are persistent as well as patient,
you can get whatever you seek."

MISTY COPELAND
BALLERINA

Susan La Flesche Picotte

1865–1915

PATHFINDING STUDENT • 1ST NATIVE AMERICAN WITH A MEDICAL DEGREE • HOSPITAL FOUNDER

When only a child, Susan La Flesche Picotte found herself tending as best she could to a very ill woman from her tribe, awaiting the local doctor who had been summoned four times but never arrived. When the woman died, Susan had the "long, hard struggle" that would define her life laid out clearly before her. She'd become the doctor who'd care for her people. The daughter of Iron Eyes, the last recognized Omaha chief, Susan readily enlisted in her father's cause—serving their tribe and preserving its culture by gaining as much knowledge as they could, both on and off their Nebraska reservation. She had already graduated from two schools and was fluent in Omaha-Ponca, English, French, and Otoe, when a fellow teacher at the Quaker Mission School—Harvard anthropologist Alice Fletcher—encouraged her to enroll at the first US university for students of color. With a diploma from Virginia's Hampton Institute, the salutatorian secured a scholarship from the Office of Indian Affairs to attend medical school. She earned her MD in 1889, a year early and at the top of her class.

Returning to the Omaha Reservation, Susan became its primary doctor and a trusted community leader. She'd brave every extreme of Great Plains weather, trekking across her 1,350-square-mile territory to conduct house calls. Besides treating long lines of patients, she was sought as a lawyer, financial adviser, and government liaison. Whenever Susan diagnosed widespread problems, she'd throw herself into public health campaigns to address them. To combat frequent bouts of cholera, she began educating on hygiene. When she saw tribal members hocking their possessions to buy whiskey, she successfully lobbied to ban liquor sales on Omaha land. In 1913, Susan finally reached the shore of her greatest ambition—opening a reservation hospital. Built entirely with proceeds from years of steadfast fundraising, the small outfit was the county's first modern medical center. The founder did not live long to serve there, but she died knowing there was a facility and staff—many of whom she had personally inspired to become doctors—to care for her people.

"I know I have a long, hard struggle before me, but the shores of success can only be reached by crossing the bridge of faith, and I shall try hard."

SUSAN LA FLESCHE PICOTTE
PHYSICIAN

Anne Sullivan

1866–1936

ILLITERATE ORPHAN TURNED STAR STUDENT • SPECIAL EDUCATION PIONEER • THE "MIRACLE WORKER"

Anne Sullivan was the ingenious educator beside Helen Keller, the deaf-blind humanitarian who became one of the 20th century's best-loved figures. Though Anne's story is often overshadowed by that of her famous pupil, her tale of tenacity is no less extraordinary. The daughter of Irish immigrants, Anne grew up in grinding poverty, losing most of her eyesight to a bacterial infection. After her mother died and her father abandoned the family, Anne was sent to a notorious almshouse where the 10-year-old lived amid society's neediest castaways in squalor and neglect. Instead of succumbing to despair, she planned a way out. When a charitable commission came to inspect the facilities, Anne interrupted their tour with a moving plea for education. In 1880, they sent her to Perkins School for the Blind. The illiterate teenager was miles behind, but she made up for it with incomparable grit, graduating as valedictorian.

When a pair of overwhelmed parents wrote the Perkins principal to plead for help with their deaf and blind 6-year-old daughter, he knew Anne was the obvious choice. She arrived in Alabama to find an unruly girl seemingly lost to the world. Attempts to instill discipline did no good. Anne realized to awaken Helen, she needed to breathe life into knowledge. Her first attempt—putting one of Helen's hands under rushing water while finger-spelling the word into her other—became a breakthrough moment. With Helen's natural curiosity dictating their curriculum, she began making giant leaps. Prominent deaf educator Alexander Graham Bell helped publicize Anne's successes. She and her wonder student were invited to meet the US president and publicly celebrated by the likes of Thomas Edison and Mark Twain. They became an inseparable duo as Anne devoted herself to Helen's ambitions, manually signing all her lectures so she could become the first deaf-blind college grad, editing her many manuscripts, and serving as Helen's voice during her extensive lecture and goodwill tours. When death finally separated them, Anne's ashes went to Washington, DC's National Cathedral as a tribute to the trailblazer who had turned halting steps into world-inspiring progress.

> " People seldom see the halting and painful steps by which the most insignificant success is achieved. "

ANNE SULLIVAN
TEACHER

Joan Bavaria

1943–2008

ARTIST TURNED BANKER • *TIME* MAGAZINE "HERO FOR THE PLANET" • SOCIALLY RESPONSIBLE INVESTING CATALYST

At 23, Joan Bavaria was an art school dropout, divorcée, and single mother of two. Badly in need of an income, profession, and new direction, she gratefully accepted an entry-level job her uncle secured for her at a Boston bank. Joan would go on to hustle her way from investment officer to leading financier with her own game-changing firm. Along the way, the environmentalist catalyzed a worldwide movement for socially responsible investing, taking it from a small-scale enterprise with a niche set of clients to the mainstream of global corporate responsibility.

Being an industry outsider helped Joan see how things could be done differently. Her interventions began early when she defied managers by establishing an on-site lunchtime exercise program for her fellow workers. It garnered a presidential commendation and national media attention as an innovative employee health initiative. It also got her an invitation to join the management program. As the maverick ascended the ranks, she became increasingly convinced of the need to carve out a space for clients who wanted investments aligned with their values. In 1982 she founded Trillium Asset Management—named after the three-petaled flower as a nod to the company's pioneering of a "triple bottom line." The first investment adviser to focus exclusively on sustainable and responsible investing, the visionary firm put into practice Joan's belief that financial decisions should be evaluated according to their social and environmental costs and benefits. When the 1989 *Exxon Valdez* oil spill went on the books as one of the worst human-caused disasters in history, Joan saw an opportunity to make her model into a movement. She cofounded the Coalition for an Environmentally Responsible Economy (CERES), calling on businesses to adopt rules of conduct and transparent reporting on environmental performance. Today, her NGO is an international network of nonprofits, businesses, and investment funds with collective assets topping $11 trillion. And the principles she pioneered have never been more relevant or widely embraced. Though the changes may sometimes be slow and incremental, Joan proved that when shareholders pay attention to where their money's going, it yields serious returns for the planet.

"I'm not deterred by lack of magnitude or lack of millions of people on the streets demonstrating; small gains are what it's all about."

JOAN BAVARIA
GREEN INVESTOR

Susan Butcher

1954–2006

MUSHER & PIONEERING DOG TRAINER • IDITAROD LEGEND & 4-TIME WINNER • DOGGED COMPETITOR

When Susan Butcher moved to Alaska at age 20, she went straight off the grid. A single-engine plane dropped her, a friend, and four puppies at a backcountry cabin with no electricity or running water. Susan's parents got the hint from her very first elementary school composition—"I hate the city. I love the country."—that she might well have a future in the great outdoors, but they could never have guessed that their Massachusetts kid would go on to become one of the greatest mushers in history. In fact, Susan was studying to become a vet tech when she read an article about the inaugural Iditarod dogsled race, a grueling 1,049-mile trek over a frozen terrain commemorating the dash to deliver diphtheria serum from Anchorage to Nome. She had an overriding vision of herself crossing the finish line as its winner. That daydream quickly became a must-do that dictated her every action, from leaving veterinary school to hurtle herself into the Alaskan outback to operating her own kennel so she could train year-round.

In 1978, the unstoppable Susan competed in her first of 16 Iditarods. She notched her first win in 1986. Her record time of 11 days, 15 hours, 6 minutes was even more impressive given that it took place just a year after a moose attack left two of her team dead and 13 injured. (She fought the moose off with her parka and an axe.) The first person with three consecutive victories, Susan's triumphs not only broke records, they changed the culture of the sport. When she started racing, her competitors thought she'd never win because she "babied" her dogs. Treating them as valued teammates, she led through mutual trust. By the time Susan retired with four Iditarod titles, her humane and nurturing training methods had become best practices. While the champion's life was cut short by leukemia, her legacy is celebrated each March with Alaska's Susan Butcher Day, and the still-active Trail Breaker Kennel where she raised two daughters and 96 huskies remains a local landmark.

"

I do not know
the word 'quit.'
Either I never did or
I have somehow
abolished it.

"

SUSAN BUTCHER
DOGSLEDDER

Ronda Rousey

born 1987

RESILIENT KID TURNED JUDO CHAMP • 1ST FEMALE UFC HALL-OF-FAMER •
ATHLETE WHO'S REDEFINING STRENGTH

One of the world's baddest ladies, fighter Ronda "Rowdy" Rousey, has serious swagger in and outside the ring. Though she now exudes unquestionable confidence on many intimidating stages from the Ultimate Fighting Championship octagon to the silver screen, there was once a time when delivering a few endlessly rehearsed lines in an elementary school play was a huge victory. Born with her umbilical cord wrapped around her neck, Ronda was left with a motor speech disorder that made everything she tried to say an unintelligible jumble. Her parents didn't know if the damage was permanent and relocated to North Dakota so she could take intensive "talking classes" with specialists. The therapy helped transform the girl who dismissed herself as dumb into one ready to conquer the world in words and in deeds. With her mother as her first trainer, Ronda would go on to become the first American to win an Olympic judo medal at the 2008 Games. Coming home with her bronze, the sixth dan black belt was dejected to find it didn't count for much. Her hunger to win still unsated, she dove into the no-holds-barred arena of mixed martial arts, sparring in the UFC's first-ever women's fight. With her phenomenal poise and well-honed technique, Ronda dominated as the UFC's bantamweight champ, keeping the belt for six epic matches and besting her opponents in an average of 2 minutes, 36 seconds.

In 2018, Ronda continued her run as a combat sports pioneer in the WWE, where the pro wrestler headlined their debut all-women's pay-per-view event. Though the all-in competitor isn't quite ready to leave the ring, she's taking her fighting spirit to new arenas—from film and TV to philanthropic work. A longtime supporter of mental health charities, in honor of her father who took his own life, Ronda has openly shared her own struggles with depression, especially after the stunning, 48-second knockout that unseated her as a UFC titleholder. She's hoping that if someone so seemingly unbreakable admits she needs backup, people will see asking for help as a sign of strength.

"You have to fight because you can't count on anyone else fighting for you. And you have to fight for people who can't fight for themselves. To get anything of real value, you have to fight for it."

RONDA ROUSEY
PROFESSIONAL WRESTLER

VALIANTLY

"Optimistic, hopeful people view barriers and obstacles as problems to be solved and not as the reason to give up or turn back. Positive people never, ever give up."

WILMA MANKILLER
CHEROKEE CHIEF

Sojourner Truth

1797–1883

RELIGIOUS & SOCIAL VISIONARY • ANTISLAVERY MISSIONARY •
NEW FACE ON THE $10 BILL

In 1863, during the height of the Civil War, Sojourner Truth was slated to speak at an Indiana town hall. She'd gone to help convert the stronghold of Southern sympathizers in a deeply divided state. When threats to burn down the venue and assassinate her rolled in, she refused to cancel her appearance or carry a weapon. Instead, Sojourner dispelled the mob by rolling into the meeting flanked by the home guard and belting "The Star-Spangled Banner." Despite multiple attempts to arrest her, she stayed there a month, waging one of her many fruitful battles for the "cause of human freedom." The 6-foot-tall evangelist for the truth had opted out of fear long before. Born into slavery, she'd been beaten, sold five times, and had four children taken away from her, escaping with her infant daughter just before New York's slavery ban took effect in 1827. In her first outing as a public speaker, she convinced a grand jury to return her 5-year-old son from bondage in Alabama. However, it wasn't until 1843 that the deeply religious Sojourner was inspired by a vision to quit her job and become a full-time servant of God. Traveling wherever the spirit called her, she spread the gospels of abolition, women's rights, and temperance.

Sojourner's booming voice and imposing presence made audiences give her a chance. Her sincere and captivating sermons held their attention and made her a legend. Invited to speak at meetings, conferences, churches, and state legislatures across the land, she attracted notable collaborators and admirers, including Susan B. Anthony, Frederick Douglass, and Abraham Lincoln. During the Civil War, the preacher turned her powers of persuasion to recruiting black troops for the Union while administering to wounded soldiers and emancipated slaves. Sojourner's larger-than-life career is memorialized with a towering bronze statue in her final resting place of Battle Creek, Michigan. The prominent suffragist also stands tall in Central Park's first-ever statue to feature real, historical women—a tribute to the centennial of women's right to vote.

I feel safe even in the midst of my enemies; for the truth is powerful and will prevail.

SOJOURNER TRUTH
PREACHER

Dorothea Dix

1802–1887

SCHOOL FOUNDER • UNION SUPERINTENDENT OF ARMY NURSES •
UNCONQUERABLE ADVOCATE

Long before women could vote or testify before Congress, Dorothea Dix was a high-impact lobby-ist, getting legislation passed and spearheading a movement that dramatically changed how we approach mental health issues. Her compassionate crusade may have been influenced by her own childhood spent with parents hampered by psychological difficulties. Eventually taken in by her afflu-ent grandmother in Boston, the bright teen became a teacher, opening a school for girls when she was only 20 years old. Prone to depressing bouts of incapacitating sickness, in 1836, Dorothea was encouraged by a physician to go recuperate in Europe. Instead of kicking back, she met with forward-thinking politicians and campaigners. Dorothea returned to the States freed from financial burdens by an inheritance from her grandmother and ready to set out as a full-time reformer. She began by touring prisons and poorhouses, reporting on the inhumane handling of the mentally ill. Massachusetts lawmakers were so moved by her harrowing testimony, they voted to create a state-run asylum for the moral treatment of patients. By 1845, Dorothea had covered more than 10,000 miles across 12 other states, successfully lobbying for the establishment of six more asylums.

As Dorothea threw all her energy behind pushing for national legislation, she suffered a devastat-ing setback. Her bill, granting 12 million acres of federal land for the creation of public care facilities, passed both houses of Congress in 1854, but was vetoed by the president. She put her gallant reac-tion down in writing—"Defeated not conquered; disappointed not discouraged." True to her words, Dorothea didn't stop. She traversed Europe to conduct a comparative care study, recommending improvements in many countries. A meeting with Pope Pius IX saw him personally direct the building of a new asylum. By the time she retired, the dauntless Dorothea had brought about the construction or expansion of 30 hospitals. Most importantly, she'd been instrumental in changing perceptions about the "insane." Instead of seeing them as lost souls requiring punishment and heavy restraint, she saw fellow humans deserving humane treatment for problems that may well be remedied.

Defeated not conquered; disappointed not discouraged.

DOROTHEA DIX
MENTAL HEALTH REFORMER

Sarah Emma Edmonds

1841–1898

FARM GIRL CHASING FREEDOM • UNION SOLDIER, NURSE & SPY • PLUCKY PATRIOT

Born on a Canadian farm, Sarah Emma Edmonds ran away to the US to escape an abusive father and forced marriage. Realizing she stood a better chance of making a living as a man, she created the persona of Franklin Flint Thompson and became a successful traveling Bible salesman. She was plying her trade in Flint, Michigan, when the Civil War broke out in 1861. Without hesitation she took her cross-dressing to the next level and enlisted in the Union army. As Private Thompson in the 2nd Michigan Regiment, Sarah saw action as a field nurse, hospital attendant, and stretcher-bearer dealing with mass casualties. She also served as a mail carrier, courier, and orderly, traversing dangerous territories and battlefields to deliver vital communications and once breaking a leg and sustaining lifelong internal injuries when her horse was fatally wounded. Besides participating in the Siege of Yorktown and Battle of Williamsburg, Sarah tapped into her well-honed knack for disguise to infiltrate Confederate troops, crossing enemy lines 11 times with as many aliases.

More soldiers were lost to sickness during the Civil War than to combat. When Sarah contracted malaria in 1863, she knew the gig was up. Instead of risking discovery, she deserted her post, reemerging as a female volunteer with the US Christian Commission where she served as a nurse till the end of the war. Even before General Lee surrendered, Sarah published her remarkable story, *Nurse and Spy in the Union Army*, donating all proceeds from the best-selling memoir to soldiers' aid charities. In 1876, Sarah, by then a wife and mother, ventured to attend the reunion of her old regiment. She was greeted with open arms by her fellow soldiers, many of whom helped her get the desertion charge erased from her record and secure a government pension. In 1897, she was likewise welcomed as the sole female member admitted into the fraternal organization for Union vets, the Grand Army of the Republic. Soon after, the brave servicewoman was laid to rest near her last home, buried with military honors at Houston's Washington Cemetery.

"I am naturally fond of adventure, a little ambitious, and a good deal romantic . . . but patriotism was the grand secret of my success."

SARAH EMMA EDMONDS
SECRET SOLDIER

Tammie Jo Shults

born 1961

NAVY OFFICER • PIONEERING COMMERCIAL PILOT •
HEROIC LIFESAVER WITH "NERVES OF STEEL"

On April 18, 2018, Southwest Airlines captain Tammie Jo Shults was 20 minutes into a routine domestic flight when the left engine on her Boeing 737-700 exploded in midair. The blast tore away a section of plane, spraying shrapnel into the wing and main cabin. One passenger, Jennifer Riordan, tragically lost her life; the rest were panicking as the cabin rapidly lost pressure and oxygen masks dropped down. While the aircraft was in chaos, shaking and steeply tilting to one side, its captain calmly communicated with air traffic control before maneuvering an emergency landing that saved 148 lives. After touchdown, Tammie Jo went up and down the aisles, personally checking on each passenger. The stunning incident made immediate headlines. The pilot didn't release her name, but her grateful passengers refused to let her heroism go unacknowledged.

As Tammie Jo's backstory came to light, people realized her whole life has been defined by a remarkable sense of duty and courage. Raised on a ranch near a New Mexico Air Force base, she'd grown up awestruck by air drills. The teen knew she wanted to serve and fly. When a colonel at a career day discouraged her from attempting, she temporarily rerouted her ambitions toward veterinary care, but couldn't shake the dream of getting into the cockpit. She tried to enlist in the Army, Air Force, and Navy, but they kept putting her off or telling her to send along her brother instead. Finally, a year after taking the Navy aviation exam, Tammie Jo found a recruiter willing to accept her. She served as an instructor and tactical pilot before being selected for the first female team to fly supersonic F/A-18 combat jets. Leaving the armed forces as a lieutenant commander, she joined Southwest as one of the first female commercial airline pilots in 1994. No doubt Tammie Jo's military training helped her meet the most high-stakes challenge of her life. Her intrepid attitude probably played its part, too. And that's why the next class of highfliers have Tammie Jo on their radar.

> "Heroes are just people who take the time to see and the effort to act on behalf of someone else."

TAMMIE JO SHULTS
PILOT

Scout Bassett

born 1988

ORPHAN • PARALYMPIC SPRINTER & LONG JUMPER •
FASTEST AMERICAN IN HER CLASS

When Scout Bassett was 18 months old, she was discovered abandoned on the streets of Nanjing, China, with burns and a badly mangled leg from a chemical fire. A month before she turned eight, a loving couple from Northern Michigan arrived to adopt her from a Chinese orphanage. They found her underweight, struggling with the aftermath of a poorly executed amputation, and hobbling around on a homemade prothesis. Scout hadn't been outdoors for six years. In the US, she received good medical care and lived a life without want, but finding her way in a small-town, all-white private school was no fairytale. The turning point came when her mother took her to be fitted for a custom prosthetic by an industry-leading expert. He looked at the slight, shy, and lost 4'9" Scout and convinced her she could be an athlete, even taking her to compete in her first Paralympic event at 14. Scout hunched over stifling sobs at the runner's blocks, but by the time she crossed the finish line (well behind the pack), her anger and terror had been replaced by a new sense of community and possibility. Running put the once-timid girl on track to forging a new identity as a tough, driven competitor.

After attending UCLA on a full ride, Scout had her first Paralympic Olympic Games in sight. That is, until she finished dead last at the qualifiers. Instead of giving up on her goal, Scout quit her day job with a medical device company to focus solely on training. It was a risky move that saw her living out of her car and surviving off ramen for months. A year after she made the leap, sponsors started to come through. In 2016, she came through for them, qualifying for Team USA and competing in the 100-meter sprint and long jump at the Rio Olympics. Scout has yet to win gold, but her odds-defying story has earned her many a fan. Now a Nike spokesperson who has been featured in ESPN's *Body Issue*, the inspiring sprinter is accelerating toward the world she'd like to see by encouraging us all to embrace our scars.

The beauty of being underestimated is that you have an opportunity to defy the odds.

SCOUT BASSETT
ATHLETE

WITTILY

"Everything in moderation,
including moderation."

JULIA CHILD
CHEF

Tallulah Bankhead

1902–1968

TEEN BROADWAY ACTOR • STAGE LEGEND • BRAZEN PUBLICITY MAGNET

Tallulah Bankhead was a stage siren known for her husky voice and propensity to call everyone "*Dah-ling.*" The first Alabama woman to rise to international celebrity, she didn't do it by becoming the genteel Southern belle her affluent family had hoped. The exuberant child—whose favorite pastime was singing and dancing for guests atop the dining room table—was so difficult to rein in that she was shipped off to convent school by the time she was 10. Tallulah rebelled, finding her own way into the limelight in 1918 by winning a movie fan magazine contest. The prize? A trip to New York and a bit part in a silent film. Once the precocious teen got a taste of showbiz, there was no stopping her ambition.

Tallulah was blessed with many advantages. She had money, beauty, and a US congressman father who could pull strings. But the secret weapon that helped her break into the industry and made her so memorable was her devastating wit. Dazzling onstage, her offstage paint-the-town-red persona was equally tantalizing. Though Tallulah charmed many artists in New York, the London stage made her a superstar. She went there for a single play in 1923 and ended up headlining 24 productions, ritually attended by a devoted posse of women who'd scream "Tallulah Hallelujah!" every time she made an entrance. A too-good-to-refuse Hollywood studio contract lured her back to the States, but she had little patience for filmmaking and longed to be back in front of live audiences. After several flops, she made a triumphant return to Broadway with acclaimed performances in classics like *The Little Foxes* and *The Skin of Our Teeth*. Her only silver-screen hit came with Alfred Hitchcock's 1944 *Lifeboat*; soon after, she found the perfect showcase for her comedic spark as the host of a popular radio variety show. But in the end, the price of being the inimitable Tallulah took its toll. As the health problems caused by her decadent lifestyle mounted, she took her last role—a memorably campy guest spot as the villainous Black Widow on TV's *Batman*.

> ❝
>
> **Nobody can be exactly like me. Sometimes even I have trouble doing it.**
>
> ❞

TALLULAH BANKHEAD
ACTOR

Betty Friedan

1921–2006

EDITOR & WRITER • COFOUNDER OF NOW • CATALYST FOR THE MODERN WOMEN'S MOVEMENT

Betty Friedan is widely recognized as the woman who set off American feminism's second big wave. She did so with inextinguishable wit and fire, revving people up and fomenting debate with memorable calls to action like: "Women of the world unite! You have nothing to lose but your vacuum cleaners." The daughter of Jewish immigrants, Betty had little chance of being one of the "cool" kids in her Peoria, Illinois, high school, but dealing with unwarranted social slights gave her the strength to face backlash later in her career. She flourished by pursuing her passion for journalism, writing for her high school newspaper and editing one in college. Fired from her job as a union newspaper editor when her second maternity leave loomed, she took up freelancing for women's magazines, snagging frequent bylines in *Redbook, Ladies Home Journal*, and *McCall's*. When her 15-year reunion at Smith College arrived, Betty pitched a piece showing how higher ed hadn't sullied her classmates' prospects for domestic bliss. Instead, her survey found most fellow alumnae were profoundly unhappy, suffering from a "problem that had no name." Betty found one for it—the "feminine mystique."

When four editors who'd always accepted her previous work turned down the story, she knew she was on to something dangerous but important. Over the next five years, Betty undertook meticulous research to convert her article into a book that explored how social institutions, from advertising to education, were conspiring to perpetuate the myth that women were domestic goddesses whose purpose could only be fulfilled through marriage and motherhood. Released in 1963, *The Feminine Mystique* became an overnight best seller and one of the most influential texts of the 20th century. Millions of women identified with the housewife malaise Betty diagnosed and felt empowered by her argument that its primary causes were rooted in social structures, not personal psychology. Capitalizing on the momentum generated by her book, Betty galvanized women and men to fight for gender equality, ushering in workplace and government policies that applied her simple principle: treat women first and foremost as people.

"I'm horrified by the word 'cool.' Coolness is an evasion of life. Being cool isn't it at all. What I think you're supposed to be is passionate, fanatic and crusading. I'd rather be hot and wrong."

BETTY FRIEDAN
FEMINIST

Julia Louis-Dreyfus

born 1961

IMPROV ACTOR • COMEDIC GEM ON BIG AND SMALL SCREENS •
FIRST LADY OF LAUGHTER

Julia Louis-Dreyfus—an undisputed comic genius. She performed her first slapstick routine (stuffing raisins up her nose) at age three, was scouted for *Saturday Night Live* before she had finished her drama degree at Northwestern, created two landmark small-screen characters, and has won more Emmy and SAG awards than any other actor in history. In 2018, her standout career was toasted with the Mark Twain Prize for American Humor. During her Kennedy Center acceptance speech, Julia admitted how crucial comedy had been, not just for her professional development, but for her personal well-being. In fact, just 12 hours after breaking the Emmy record for most wins by a performer—nabbing the Lead Actress in a Comedy Series category for an unprecedented sixth year running—she was diagnosed with stage II breast cancer. Julia was forced to take two years off to undergo a double mastectomy and six rounds of chemo. Her family and friends kept her going with the best therapy—laughter. Sure, she was "a pretty easy audience" in her heavily medicated state, but the ordeal nonetheless reaffirmed for her how humor is a basic human need . . . "along with love and food and an HBO subscription."

In spite of her genius, Julia wasn't an overnight success. Her 1982 initiation into TV at *SNL* often felt like a hazing ritual. Too earnest and naive for the cutthroat dressing rooms of 30 Rock, she left the flagship show after just a few seasons. She was in her 30s when she became a household name as *Seinfeld*'s delightfully cynical ex-turned-bestie Elaine Benes. Her character wasn't part of the original 1989 concept, but producers insisted on adding a female lead to the hilariously flawed foursome, and Julia helped make the long-running sitcom one of the most popular and influential shows of all time. The sidesplitting frontwoman scored another critical darling and fan favorite show with the 2012 political satire *Veep*. Seven seasons later, the self-serving, gaffe-prone Selina Meyer has officially been booted from the Oval Office and safely laid to rest, but Julia's still going strong.

"

There's no situation—
none—that isn't improved
with a couple of laughs.

"

JULIA LOUIS-DREYFUS
ACTOR

Sara Blakely

born 1971

GIRL WHO DARED TO FAIL • BUSINESS MOGUL •
YOUNGEST SELF-MADE FEMALE BILLIONAIRE

Before Sara Blakely had her billion-dollar idea for Spanx, she had plenty of nonstarters. She wanted to be a lawyer but bombed the LSAT—twice. She put herself out there as a stand-up comic but couldn't make a go of it. She joined the cast at Disney World but quit a few months in. Sara had been prepped for these disappointments. Her father made asking what she'd failed at into normal dinner-table conversation. He met every embarrassing anecdote with a high-five to keep her trying. And the budding entrepreneur did, eventually rolling $5,000 and a cavalcade of "nos" into a thriving global brand. In 1998, Sara was working as a fax machine salesperson when a personal wardrobe conundrum—what to wear under white slacks with sandals that wouldn't show panty lines—set off a hosiery revolution. With two snips of a scissors, she made her first prototype for an undergarment that didn't exist: footless, body-shaping pantyhose. The patent lawyer she consulted thought the idea was so wacky he feared it was a *Candid Camera* hoax. A series of male mill owners likewise rejected her concept—until one conferred with his daughters. She had to travel to Texas and haul a Neiman Marcus buyer into the ladies room for a demo to land her first account, but when Oprah named Spanx as one of her "Favorite Things," Sara knew she was finally being taken seriously.

If grit got Spanx off the ground, Sara's sense of humor got it soaring. After all, she never expected her own butt would be the inspiration for a business empire. She used that comic origin story, along with sassy-fun marketing and punny product names to score press hits and generate buzz when she couldn't afford advertising. Today, the queen of shapewear is devoting herself to reshaping the world. Besides pledging to donate at least half her fortune, she's ensuring that thousands more female entrepreneurs hear "yes!" instead of "no." A muse and mentor to many, Sara's spreading the gospel of embracing failure with her witty reminder: "The worst thing that can happen is you become memorable."

"

Humor is important. I don't believe you have to act serious to be taken seriously.

"

SARA BLAKELY
ENTREPRENEUR

Tiffany Haddish

born 1979

**FOSTER KID • 1ST BLACK WOMAN STAND-UP TO HOST *SNL* •
DISARMINGLY AUTHENTIC "SOUL TICKLER"**

Even for Tiffany Haddish, her story borders on unbelievable. A breakout comedy star following her scene-stealing performance in the 2017 summer gut-buster *Girls Trip,* it took her more than 20 years to get there. The South-Central LA native launched herself onto the circuit fresh out of high school. Here and there, she'd clown her way into the spotlight, with a comedy competition or sitcom guest spot, but mostly she scraped by as an all-around "energy producer" for events, weddings, and over 500 bar mitzvahs, earning so little she was frequently forced to live out of her tiny car. Her path to comedy was also less than rosy. After her mother sustained brain damage in a car crash, Tiffany grew up in the foster care system, bouncing between caretakers and group homes, carrying around her few belongings in a garbage bag that made her feel like trash. By the time she was a teen, she'd become a determined troublemaker with a knack for making her class-mates laugh. A social worker finally issued an ultimatum: she could either spend her summer in psychiatric treatment or in a Laugh Factory camp for underprivileged kids. Tiffany chose the latter. Her inner stand-up saved her life.

The survivor's tough-luck start and willingness to put her "funny, honest, hot mess" of a self out there are what make her act so compelling. She's brought her trademark bluntness to every-thing from a best-selling memoir to an exclusive comedy special. Her crowd-winning performance hosting *Saturday Night Live*—the first African American female stand-up to do so—earned her an Emmy, along with a host of other film and TV roles. Now fast friends with A-list celebs whose mansions she once randomly parked her car outside of to sleep, Tiffany's also a talk show favorite for her raucous storytelling and propensity to spill the beans about her vaunted social circle. As her star rises, she wants to help other foster kids map their own improbable stories. For a start, she's giving them suitcases, so they never have to feel like they're being taken out with the trash.

For real,
that happened?

TIFFANY HADDISH
COMEDIAN

Now get the hell out of here and go change the world.

"

LUCILLE BALL
COMEDIAN

SOURCE IT!

Authentically

Ferrera, America. "My identity is a superpower—not an obstacle." TED2019, April 2019. https://www.ted.com/talks/america_ferrera_my_identity_is_a_superpower_not_an_obstacle.

Gulick, Amy. "Salmon in the Trees." WildSpeak Presentation 2016. iLCP, February 8, 2017. https://vimeo.com/203138235.

Hale, Sarah Josepha. "The First Swallow," *Three Hours: Or, the Vigil of Love and Other Poems*. Cary & Hart, 1848.

Lewis, Edna. "What is Southern?" *Gourmet Magazine*, January 2008.

Oakley, Annie. Postcard (1922). Quoted in Shirl Kasper's *Annie Oakley*. University of Oklahoma Press, 2007, 232.

Boldly

Cooney, Joan Ganz. Quoted in Cary O'Dell's *Women Pioneers in Television*. McFarland & Company, Inc., 1997, 68.

Mink, Patsy. Interview. *Honolulu Star Bulletin*, October 8, 1975.

Nguyen, Amanda. "Rise CEO Amanda Nguyen on Launching a Civil Rights Startup that Fights for Rape Survivors." Profile by Tanya Klich. *Forbes*, March 8, 2019.

Ride, Sally. Interview. *All Things Considered*. NPR, February 2, 2003.

Smith, Bessie. Quoted in Nat Hentoff's *Jazz Is*. Random House, 1976.

Bravely

Biles, Simone. "Simone Biles on How She Went From Foster Care to Olympic Gold." Interview with Shaun Dreisbach. *Glamour Women of the Year*, November 1, 2016.

Hall, Virginia. Letter. Quoted in Elizabeth McIntosh's *Sisterhood of Spies*. Naval Institute Press, 1998.

Lewis, Ida. Quoted in Lenore Skomal's *The Keeper of Lime Rock*. Running Press, 2002, 24.

Tubman, Harriet. Quoted in Ednah Dow Cheney's "Moses." *Freedman's Record*, March 1865.

Williams, Jody. "Jody Williams on peace." Video. Nobel Prize, December 3, 2013. https://www.youtube.com/watch?v=BBJIKsuy4Ug.

Candidly

Ginsburg, Ruth Bader. "The Place of Women on the Court." Interview. *New York Times Magazine*, July 7, 2009.

Landers, Ann. *Wake Up and Smell the Coffee!* Random House, 1998.

Mock, Janet. *Redefining Realness*. Atria Books, 2014.

Perkins, Frances. "Labor Under the New Deal and the New Frontier." Lecture series. UCLA, 1963.

Wells, Ida B. Quoted in *The Light of Truth: Writings of an Anti-Lynching Crusader*. Eds. Mia Bay and Henry Louis Gates Jr. Penguin Books, 2014.

Compassionately

Edelman, Marian Wright. Quoted in Sheryl Grana's *Women and Justice*. Rowman & Littlefield, 2010, 104.

Keller, Elisabeth. Profile. RSF Social Finance, 2017. https://rsfsocialfinance.org/person/elisabeth-keller/.

Novogratz, Jacqueline. "Inspiring a life of immersion." TEDWomen, 2010. https://www.ted.com/talks/jacqueline_novogratz_inspiring_a_life_of_immersion.

Roosevelt, Eleanor. "My Day." *My Day*, United Feature Syndicate, Inc, December 22, 1945.

Winnemucca, Sarah. *Life Among the Piutes: Their Wrongs and Claims*. JP Putnam's Sons, 1883.

Creatively

Gang, Jeanne. *Reveal: Studio Gang Architects*. Princeton Architectural Press, 2011.

Moreno, Rita. "32nd Annual Nancy Hanks Lecture." Americans for the Arts, March 4, 2019.

Price, Florence. "Keep Your Ideals in Front of You, They Will Lead to Victory, says Mrs. Florence B. Price." Interview with Goldie Walden. *The Chicago Defender*, July 11, 1936, 7.

Shaughnessy, Dawn. "In Situ with Dawn Shaughnessy." Interview with Kit Chapman. *Chemistry World*, March 26, 2019.

Wong, Alice. "Resistance & Hope: An Interview with Alice Wong." Nicola Griffith, October 16, 2018. https://nicolagriffith.com/2018/10/16/resistance-hope-an-interview-with-alice-wong/.

Daringly

Bigelow, Kathryn. "Kathryn Bigelow discusses role of 'seductive violence' in her films." Interview with Michelle Perry. *The Tech at MIT*, March 16, 1990.

Clark, Eugenie. "An Interview with Eugenie Clark." Interview with E.K. Balon. *Women in Ichthyology*. Springer Science+Business Media, 1994, 124.

Lauder, Estée. *Estée: A Success Story*. Random House, 1985, 221.

McCluggage, Denise. Quoted in *Women Sports Magazine*, June 1977, 18.

Peck, Annie Smith. Quoted in *Women Sports*, 1977, Volume 4, 49.

Faithfully

Chodron, Thubten. *Buddhism for Beginners.* Shambhala Publications, 2001.

Harjo, Joy. *Crazy Brave.* WW Norton & Co, 2012.

Seton, Elizabeth Ann. *The Collected Writings of Elizabeth Ann Bayley Seton.* Ed. Regina Bechtle. New City Press, 2000.

Williams, Terry Tempest. "Wild Mercy." *Voice in the Wilderness: Conversations with Terry Tempest.* Ed. Michael Austin. Utah State University Press, 2006.

Winfrey, Oprah. "Harry's Last Lecture on a Meaningful Life." Stanford Divinity School, April 21, 2015.

Fiercely

Alcott, Louisa May. *Little Women.* Roberts Brothers, 1868.

Apgar, Virginia. Profile. The Virginia Apgar Papers, the US National Library of Medicine. https://profiles.nlm.nih.gov/spotlight/cp/feature/biographical-overview. Accessed October 2019.

Beyoncé. Quoted in "Chloe x Halle Are Taking Over the Industry with this Solid Advice from Beyoncé." Article by Danielle Kwateng-Clark. *Essence*, May 8, 2017.

Hamer, Fannie Lou. "We're On Our Way." Speech. Negro Baptist School of Indianola, MS, September 1964.

Jones, Mary Harris. Speech. Quoted in Elliot Gorn's *Mother Jones: The Most Dangerous Woman in America.* Hall and Wang, 2015, 3.

Freely

Aden, Halima. "Meet Halima Aden." Interview with Ellie Pithers. *Vogue UK*, April 19, 2018.

Coachman, Alice. "Black History Minute." City of Inglewood CA, February 11, 2019. https://archive.org/details/cica-Black_History_Minute-_Alice_Coachman_Davis.

Daggett, Hallie. "A Woman as a Forest Fire Lookout." *American Forestry*, Volume XX. The American Forestry Association, 1914, 178.

Earhart, Amelia. *Last Flight.* Ed. George Putnam. Putnam, 1937.

Shaw, Ruth Faison. Ruth Faison Shaw Exhibit. The Chapel Hill Museum, North Carolina Digital Collections. http://digital.ncdcr.gov/cdm/ref/collection/p16062coll8/id/3373.

Gracefully

Ash, Aesha. "Why Aesha Ash is Wandering Around Inner City Rochester in a Tutu." Article by Jennifer Stahl. *Dance Magazine*, January 11, 2017.

Chenery, Penny. "Racing Royalty." Profile by Lenny Shulman. *BloodHorse*, September 23, 2017.

Malone, Annie. Commencement address. Poro Gardens, Chicago, July 1, 1956.

Morgan, Julia. Letter to Phoebe Hearst (1898). Quoted in "Julia Morgan and the Monday Club." Article by Will Peischel. *Mustang News*, October 18, 2016.

Onassis, Jacqueline Kennedy. Oral history interview with Terry Birdwhistell. *The Kentucky Review*, 1990.

Honorably

Adams, Abigail. Letter to John Quincy Adams, June 10, 1778.

Comerford, Cristeta. "What's it like to feed the most powerful man in the world?" Profile by Sheena McKenzie. Leading Women, CNN, September 16, 2014.

Nooyi, Indra. "Stay calm during turbulent times." *The Hindu*, November 15, 2013.

Smith, Margaret Chase. "A Declaration of Conscience." Speech. US Congress, June 1, 1950.

Walker, Dr. Mary. Letter to the editor. *The Sibyl*, 1862.

Ingeniously

Blair, Mary. Quoted in *Magic, Color, Flair: The World of Mary Blair*. Special exhibition curated by John Canemaker. The Walt Disney Family Museum, March 13, 2014.

de la Peña, Nonny. "The future of news? Virtual reality." TEDWomen, 2015. https://www.ted.com/talks/nonny_de_la_pena_the_future_of_news_virtual_reality/.

Graham, Martha. Quoted in Agnes De Mille's *Martha: The Life and Work of Martha Graham*. Vintage Books, 1991.

Hamilton, Margaret. "NASA Engineers and Scientists: Transforming Dreams into Reality." Profile by AJS Rayl. NASA, October 16, 2008.

Willard, Emma. "Plan for Improving Female Education." J.W. Copeland, 1819.

Passionately

Carter, Ruth E. Commencement address. Suffolk University, May 19, 2019.

Ellis, Jill. Interview. FIFA Football Conference, September 22, 2019.

Hutcheson, Hilary. "Fly Fishing TV Host Stays Cool Amid Glitches." Article by Brett French. *Billings Gazette*, March 26, 2015.

Lazarus, Emma. "Work." Poem in *The Book of Sorrow*. Ed. Andrew Macphail. Oxford University Press, 1916.

Vanderbilt, Gloria. "Talking Dirty with Gloria Vanderbilt." Interview with Jessica Bennett. *Newsweek*, July 8, 2009.

Profoundly

Bancroft, Ann. "On Thin Ice." Profile by Cheryl Dahle. *Fast Company*, September 1, 2004.

Bouman, Katie. "How to take a picture of a black hole." TEDxBeaconStreet, 2016. https://www.ted.com/talks/katie_bouman_what_does_a_black_hole_look_like/.

Mason, Biddy. Personal motto passed down to her children. Quoted in *Encyclopedia of Local History*. Ed. Amy Wilson. Rowman & Littlefield, 2017.

Morrison, Toni. Commencement address. Rutgers, May 17, 2011.

Moses, Grandma. *Grandma Moses: My Life's History*. Harper, 1952.

Purposely

Cavness, Emily Núñez. "Emily Nunez Cavness: Changing the Lives of Veterans." *we represent*, September 2018.

Idár, Jovita. "Debemos Trabajar." *La Crónica*, 1911.

Parton, Dolly. *My Life and Other Unfinished Business*. HarperCollins, 1994.

Robinette, Beth. Social media post. Instagram @lazyrranch, June 30, 2019.

Rowland, Pleasant. "Pleasant Rowland: Founder and President, Pleasant Company." *Forbes Great Minds of Business*. Ed. Gretchen Morgenson. Forbes, Inc, 1997.

Resourcefully

Acevedo, Sylvia. "A Call to Lead." Podcast with Jennifer Morgan, July 8, 2019. https://acalltolead.libsyn.com/sylvia-acevedo.

Alsop, Marin. "Conversations on Creative Leadership." George Washington University School of Business, August 26, 2013. https://www.youtube.com/watch?v=FNMXBkHFqNA.

Cannon, Annie Jump. "The Henry Draper Memorial." Harvard College Observatory, 1915.

Cejas, Amelia Morán. "From Grape Picker to Wine Maker." TEDxFruitvale, November 11, 2011. https://www.youtube.com/watch?v=Sz_twtfRakU.

Stewart, Martha. *The Martha Rules*. Random House, 2006.

Tenaciously

Bavaria, Joan. "Heart of Gold: A Forum on Socially Responsible Investing." *Mother Jones Magazine*, May 1988, 52.

Butcher, Susan. Interview. The Academy of Achievement, 1991. https://www.achievement.org/achiever/susan-butcher/.

Picotte, Susan La Flesche. "My Childhood and Womanhood." Salutatorian address. Hampton Normal and Agricultural Institute, 1886.

Rousey, Ronda. *My Fight / Your Fight*. Regan Arts, 2015.

Sullivan, Anne. Letter (October 30, 1887). Helen Keller Archive, The American Foundation for the Blind.

Valiantly

Bassett, Scout. "Tips to Overcome Personal Struggles and Achieve Goals." *StatePoint*, September 27, 2016.

Dix, Dorothea. Letter (March 1851). *The Lady and the President: Letters of Dorothea Dix and Millard Fillmore*. Ed. Charles Snyder. The University of Kentucky Press, 1975.

Edmonds, Sarah Emma. *Nurse and Spy in the Union Army*. DeWolfe, Fiske & Co, 1864.

Shults, Tammie Jo. Heal Our Patriots. Samaritan's Purse, July 2019.

Truth, Sojourner. *Narrative of Sojourner Truth*. Review and Herald Office, 1884.

Wittily

Bankhead, Tallulah. *Tallulah: My Autobiography*. University Press of Mississippi, 1952.

Blakely, Sara. "Portrait of 25 leading American business innovators." Profile by Stephanie Mehta. *Fast Company*, January 16, 2019.

Dreyfus, Julia Louis. Acceptance speech. The 21st Annual Mark Twain Prize for American Humor. The Kennedy Center, October 21, 2018.

Friedan, Betty. "Betty Friedan's Pet Pique: The Feminine Mystique." *Life*, Vol. 55, No. 18, November 1, 1963.

Haddish, Tiffany. *The Last Black Unicorn*. Simon & Schuster, 2017.

BRAVELY HISTORYMAKERS BY STATE

We've picked quoteurs whose stories span all 50 states, plus the District of Columbia and Puerto Rico. While we can't record all the places the lives of these remarkable Americans have touched, this index provides a glimpse to help you begin mapping where they were born, blazed trails, or left their mark.

Louisiana
Elisabeth Keller

Maine
Dorothea Dix, Frances Perkins, Margaret Chase Smith

Maryland
Marin Alsop, Eugenie Clark, Virginia Hall, Annie Oakley, Elizabeth Ann Seton, Harriet Tubman

Massachusetts
Abigail Adams, Louisa May Alcott, Joan Bavaria, Katie Bouman, Susan Butcher, Annie Jump Cannon, Ruth E. Carter, Dorothea Dix, Amelia Earhart, Margaret Hamilton, Anne Sullivan

Michigan
Scout Bassett, Sarah Emma Edmonds, Sojourner Truth

Minnesota
Halima Aden, Ann Bancroft

Mississippi
Marian Wright Edelman, Fannie Lou Hamer, Biddy Mason, Ida B. Wells, Oprah Winfrey

Missouri
Annie Turnbo Malone

Montana
Hilary Hutcheson

Nebraska
Susan La Flesche Picotte

Nevada
Sarah Winnemucca

New Hampshire
Sarah Josepha Hale

New Jersey
Dorothea Dix, Toni Morrison, Martha Stewart

New Mexico
Sylvia Acevedo, Joy Harjo, Tammie Jo Shults

New York
Marin Alsop, Virginia Apgar, Aesha Ash, Tallulah Bankhead, Kathryn Bigelow, Emily Núñez Cavness, Penny Chenery, Eugenie Clark, Joan Ganz Cooney, Ruth Bader Ginsburg, Martha Graham, Beyoncé Knowles, Estée Lauder, Emma Lazarus, Edna Lewis, Julia Louis-Dreyfus, Janet Mock, Rita Moreno, Grandma Moses, Jacqueline Novogratz, Jacqueline Kennedy Onassis, Frances Perkins, Eleanor Roosevelt, Elizabeth Ann Seton, Sojourner Truth, Harriet Tubman, Gloria Vanderbilt, Mary Edwards Walker

North Carolina
Annie Oakley, Ruth Faison Shaw

North Dakota
Ronda Rousey

Ohio
Simone Biles, Toni Morrison, Annie Oakley

Oklahoma
Mary Blair, Joy Harjo

Oregon
Ann Bancroft, Hilary Hutcheson, Sarah Winnemucca

Pennsylvania
Louisa May Alcott, Martha Graham

Puerto Rico
Rita Moreno

Rhode Island
Ida Lewis, Annie Smith Peck

South Carolina
Marian Wright Edelman

South Dakota
Sylvia Acevedo

Tennessee
Mother Jones, Dolly Parton, Bessie Smith, Ida B. Wells

Texas
Simone Biles, Sarah Emma Edmonds, Jovita Idár, Beyoncé Knowles, Tammie Jo Shults, Jody Williams

Utah
Terry Tempest Williams

Vermont
Emma Willard, Jody Williams

Virginia
Jill Ellis, Edna Lewis, Grandma Moses

Washington
Thubten Chodron, Amy Gulick, Beth Robinette

Washington, DC
Abigail Adams, Cristeta Comerford, Marian Wright Edelman, Patsy Mink, Amanda Nguyen, Jacqueline Kennedy Onassis, Frances Perkins, Eleanor Roosevelt, Margaret Chase Smith

West Virginia
Mother Jones

Wisconsin
Ann Landers/Eppie Lederer, Pleasant Rowland

Wyoming
Terry Tempest Williams

GRATEFULLY

A wholehearted thank you to our champions, collaborators & muses:

All love to our families (we couldn't do it without you) . . .
Roger, Shawn & Lexi Weger • Rich, Beata & Rosie Renehan • Kathleen, Bob,
Bill & Jen • Peter, Rosa & Meridel Riley • Wendy & Peter Williamson • Claudia Riley

We wouldn't be where we are without our angels & advisers . . .
Donna Morea • Ken Bartee • Sharon Schaaf • Lisa Mascolo •
Justin & Deb Dunie • Linda Kent • Megan Beyer • Bill Tyler

Heaps of gratitude to Quotabelle's family of believers, many going back
to the early days when we were just noodling with an idea . . .
Tammy Williams • Sharon Bertschi • Shirley Kappa • Sally Browne •
Emily Williams • David Kent • Susie Bonvouloir • Liz Hamner • Megan Miller
Brawley • Alix Nunan • Kathy Lynch • Kristy Fallica • Rashin Kheiriyeh •
Chenise Williams • Angela Willard • Shelagh Bolger • James Protzman •
Jaime Wolfe • Sydney Morgan • Jim Gatto • Steve Meltzer • Justin Marcucci &
the Nickelfish team • Tom Cocuzza • Christopher Miller • Larry Yanowitch •
Lindsay Thomas • Adrianne Haslet • Tate Gillman Beaudouin

Sincerest appreciation to our editor, publisher & book designer
at Running Press, RP Studio, and Hachette Book Group . . .
Shannon Connors Fabricant • Kristin Kiser • Frances Soo Ping Chow

Then there's our literary agents extraordinaire,
who champion, cheer & occasionally coax . . .
Alexis Hurley • Kim Witherspoon • Maria Whelan

A big hats off to our collaborators . . .

We're indebted to the National Women's History Museum for their early interest in and collaboration on this project. We're huge supporters of NWHM's work to give women their rightful place in history and, with new CEO Holly Hotchner at the helm, build a meaning-filled museum in the heart of our nation's capital. A special shoutout to Lori Ann Terjesen and Liz Eberlein, Kerri Lee Alexander, and the team of NWHM staffers for their thorough research and thoughtful contributions to shaping *Bravely*'s content.

We remain in awe of the heroic leaders—Major General Dee McWilliams (US Army, retired) and Major General Jan Edmunds (US Army, retired)—who provided input on behalf of the Women In Military Service For America Memorial, located in Arlington, Virginia, the only national memorial dedicated to honoring the brave servicewomen who have defended America throughout history.

EVER THANKFUL!
PAULINE & ALICIA

Quotabelle®

We discover the ideas and stories
of real women & girls.
And make them shareable.

To spark innovation. To create connections.
To bring balance to the world.

discover her story & share her quotes
Quotabelle.com • @Quotabelle

Pauline Weger

STORYTELLER • CITESEER • SOCIAL ENTREPRENEUR

Pauline loves discovering creative ways to share inspiring ideas and true stories. She believes the world is filled with great female role models—you just need to know where to find them. It's why she founded Quotabelle.

Bravely is Pauline's fourth book. Her writing has appeared in the *Washington Post*, and she has been featured in the *Sunday Washington Post Magazine* as well as on NPR and Voice of America.

Pauline grew up in Manchester-by-the-Sea, a small coastal town north of Boston. She, her husband, and a West Highland White Terrier named Max recently moved to western Massachusetts after 25+ years living in Northern Virginia. Mom to two daughters, she stepped away from corporate life to spend her days bringing balance to the world.

Alicia Williamson

STORYTELLER • CITESEER • CHIEF EDITOR

Dr. Alicia Williamson is an author-activist and feminist educator who loves to use her keyboard for good. Since earning her PhD in literature and women's studies, she has served as a university lecturer, community organizer, and editor.

Whatever the context or medium, Alicia's work is dedicated to amplifying under-represented voices. She's delighted to be finding engaging new ways to do just that as a core member of the Quotabelle team. Her writings have been published by Wiley, Cambridge University Press, Quarto, and Running Press. *Bravely* is Alicia's fourth book with Quotabelle.

Originally from the Lake Country of Northern Minnesota, she now resides in Northeast England with her husband and their wily, wonderful brood—two young daughters and a border collie named Pony.